60 Days Praying for America

Tom Dole

Ginosko House

Flowood, MS

60 Days Praying for America

60 Days Praying for America
Copyright © 2020 by **Ginosko House Publishing**

All rights reserved. No part of this publication may be reproduced, distributed or transmitted in any form or by any means, without prior written permission.

Ginosko House LLC
316 Northshore Pl
Brandon MS 39047
www.ginoskohouse.com

All Scripture verses are from the New King James Version of the Holy Bible.

60 Days Praying for America -- 1st ed.

60 Days Praying for America

Contents

A Note From The Author 1

Devotionals

Day 1 - Population Subset 7
Day 2 – CINO's and the Veneer Problem 10
Day 3 – Turning America Upside-Down! 13
Day 4 – The Hand That Feeds You 16
Day 5 – A Second Revolution 19
Day 6 – Fools & Folly: A Shot In The Foot 23
Day 7 – An Easy Lesson 26
Day 8 – Primary voter Problems 30
Day 9 – Got Apples? 33
Day 10 – Manners & Self-Government 36
Day 11 – Kiss and Make Up 39
Day 12 – America's Heart Problem 43
Day 13 – Separation & Restitution 46
Day 14 – Same Heart, Same Mind 50
Day 15 – Polar Opposites 54
Day 16 – The Art of Kneeling 57
Day 17 – Heart Disease 60
Day 18 – Root Cuttings 63
Day 19 – Those Who Burn Incense 66

60 Days Praying for America

Day 20 - Crickets 69
Day 21 – You Get What you Pay For.. 72
Day 22 – What Would Happen If….. 75
Day 23 – Diluted & Deluded…... 79
Day 24 – Sum Of All Fears 82
Day 25 – Sowing Seed 86
Day 26 – Oil & Water 89
Day 27 – Lights & Baskets 94
Day 28 – Kindergartners vs. Judges – Heads Up! 97
Day 29 – Dreams & Kingdoms 100
Day 30 – To Acquire & Secure 104
Day 31 – Lowering This Raises That 107
Day 32 – Not the Same 110
Day 33 – "What Difference Does It Make?"....................................... 113
Day 34 – Pluralism Never Unites.. 116
Day 35 – Entropy & Hall Closets.. 119
Day 36 – Let the river Flow!... 122
Day 37 – Get Woke! … or Caught Napping.. 125
Day 38 – Unprotected – Womb & Pulpit 128
Day 39 – Wasting Resources 131
Day 40 – Character Of A Generation 134
Day 41 – It's An Inside Job... 137
Day 42 – Read All About It!... 140
Day 43 – Genuinely Overcoming Stupidity 143

60 Days Praying for America

Day 44 – Church Preserves..146

Day 45 – Counterfeit Character..150

Day 46 – Gravity Works..153

Day 47 – Enslaved..157

Day 48 – Your Nose Looks Funny..160

Day 49 – Draining The Right Swamp...................................164

Day 50 – Dreams & Nightmares..167

Day 51 – Restoring Order In A Chaotic America..................171

Day 52 – Absolutes Cannot Be Arbitrated............................174

Day 53 – It Is What I Say It Is..177

Day 54 – On Its Ear..180

Day 55 – Principle #7...183

Day 56 – Indispensable Alliances..186

Day 57 – Revolution Against Tyranny..................................189

Day 58 – Restoration: Love Where You Live.......................192

Day 59 – Truth or Consequences..195

Day 60 – Now You Know How..199

Addendum A

Prayer Prepper's Call To Action, Part 1................................203

Prayer Prepper's Call To Action, Part 2................................207

Prayer Prepper's Call To Action, Part 3................................211

Election Day: Truest Friend...215

Addendum B
Thanksgiving Day: Are You A Pilgrim? 219

Addendum C
Scriptures 223

End Notes 229

60 Days Praying for America

60 Days Praying for America

A NOTE FROM THE AUTHOR

Reader! Whoever you are, remember this!
The Donkey and the Elephant can't help anyone.
It's time to return to the Lamb!

These Scripture verses should be primary resources used to encourage Christian believers to pray for America:

Turn the people to the Lord their God,
turn the hearts of the fathers to the children,
turn the disobedient to the wisdom of the just…
make ready a people prepared for the Lord.[1]

We make our prayer before the LORD our God,
that we might turn from our iniquities
and understand Your truth.[2]

Lord, turn Your hand upon us,
and purely purge away our dross,
and take away all our mixture,
… restore our judges as at the first,
and our counselors as at the beginning.
Then wisdom and knowledge
shall be the stability of our times,
and strength of salvation:
the fear of the LORD is our treasure.[3]

60 Days Praying for America

The men and women who helped establish the Constitutional Republic of America's government had the unique understanding that freedom cannot be bestowed upon a person by any government. They were aware of the truth that freedom never begins with government rules and regulations. They knew that freedom is never achieved by debate and mutual consent among men. Rather they knew that freedom begins in the hearts of men. If a man is not free on the inside, he will never be free on the outside.

America's Founding Fathers were correct in their understanding that the affairs of government flow out of men's hearts. If the heart is corrupt, the fruit will be corrupt. If the heart is virtuous, the fruit will be virtuous.[4]

His Word was in my heart like a burning fire.[5] For the Founding Fathers, the fire of freedom burning in their heart was fueled by the Word of God. Their constant exhortation to individual Americans was to protect and maintain that flame in their hearts. The Founders knew that if the fire of God's Word burned pure and strong in people's hearts, then America's government would remain pure and strong. They were also well aware of the consequences should that flame diminish or burn out. What's the matchstick that starts a fire of revival in your heart? It should be the Word of God.

> "Whether this [the American Revolution] will provoke a blessing or a curse will depend upon the use our people make of the blessings which a gracious God has bestowed on us. If they are wise, they will be great and happy. If they are of a contrary character, they will be miserable. Righteousness alone can exalt them as a nation."[6]

It was Patrick Henry who warned all Americans:

60 Days Praying for America

"Righteousness alone can exalt [America] as a nation. Reader! - whoever you are, remember this! - and in your sphere practice virtue yourself, and encourage it in others. The great pillars of all government are virtue, morality, and religion. This is the armor, my friend, and this alone, that renders us invincible."[7]

Too many Americans have abandoned the armor that renders us invincible – virtue, morality, and the religion of Christianity. This armor, and the ability to live by it, can only be found in the pages of the Bible. Regretfully, the promotion, teaching, and proclamation of the Word of God has been abandoned in America in a far-to-large degree. The Bible and its teachings are no longer welcome in schools, the halls of government, the judiciary, nor in society-at-large. There are even some churches that rely on the Words of the Bible far-to-little.

It is time for a second revolution in America. Not a revolution of weapons and arms, but a revolution that takes place in the hearts of men and women. A revolution in men's hearts caused by the fire of the Word of God. A revolution where men and women truly seek God for the purpose of coming to the knowledge of His Truth.

Jesus Himself made two comments regarding this kind of revolution. First, He declared that real truth is only found in God's Word: *Father, sanctify them by Your truth, Your Word is Truth.*[8] Second, He said that it is the truth we know and live by that will set us free: *If you abide in My word, you are My disciples indeed. And you shall know the truth, and the truth shall make you free.*[9] Conversely, if we do not know and live by the truth found in God's Word, we will be enslaved by our own human nature. The more a government needs to control human nature, the more tyrannical it becomes. Then liberty is lost.

60 Days Praying for America

Just as in the days and years leading up to the founding of the United States of America, this revolution must begin with prayer! America gained its independence and freedom only through prayer, living a life of obedience to the moral teachings of the Bible, and promoting the teaching of the Bible. And this is the only means of restoring and maintaining that liberty and freedom. Our freedom and liberty come from God. It makes no sense to seek liberty and freedom from some other source. It just isn't there. We must seek freedom and liberty from God, the God of the Bible.

Are you ready to join this second revolution? If so, then,

Reader! Whoever you are, remember This!

Do not put your trust in princes,
nor in a so of man, in whom there is no help.
His spirit departs, he returns to his earth;
in that very day his plans perish.[10]

The Donkey and the Elephant can't help anyone.
It's time to return to the Lamb!

We make our prayer before the LORD our God,
that we might turn from our iniquities
and understand Your truth.[11]

Lord, turn Your hand upon us,
and purely purge away our dross,
and take away all our mixture,
... restore our judges as at the first,
and our counselors as at the beginning.
Then wisdom and knowledge
shall be the stability of our times,
and strength of salvation:
the fear of the LORD is our treasure.[12]

60 Days Praying for America

*Turn the people to the Lord their God,
turn the hearts of the fathers to the children,
turn the disobedient to the wisdom of the just…
make ready a people prepared for the Lord.*[13]

Please! Pray for America on a regular basis.

Don't live in America? Pray for your own country. These same principles work in any nation.

60 Days Praying for America

DAY 1

Population Subset

> "We call ours a Christian civilization, a Christian conception of justice. Our civilization cannot survive materially unless it be redeemed spiritually. It can be saved only by becoming permeated with the Spirit of Christ and being made free and happy by the practices which spring out of that Spirit."[1]

> "There is another enemy at home… that mocks at ideals, sneers at sacrifice and pretends that the American people can live by bread alone. If the Spirit of God is not in us, and if we will not prepare to give all we have and all that we are to preserve Christian civilization in our land, we shall go to destruction."[2]

THESE INSIGHTFUL COMMENTS were made by, of all people, two Democrats. How nice it would be if today's Democrats – and Republicans! – would refresh their memories and value systems. Among America's Founding Fathers there was not one who failed to understand that the moment a society loses biblical Christianity as the moral anchor of its character and nature, then both the government and the nation will fall into ruin. *Righteousness exalts a nation, but sin is a reproach to any people.*[3]

John Adams declared that the principles upon which America's founders established independence were the 'general principles of Christianity.' He further stated that those principles were 'eternal and immutable.'[4] That means that any nation past, present, or future can gain its independence if it will establish the principles of biblical Christianity as the basis of its culture and society.

In any society, God's desire is government and civil order. God is opposed to lawlessness, anarchy, rebellion, and wickedness. Why does God desire the one and oppose the other? Because in every culture and society He wants there to be enough calm and tranquility to allow people to freely consider His ways, His truths, and to come to know Him.[5]

Unfortunately, human nature being what it is, there will always be those motivated by jealousy, greed, and personal ambition who will oppose God's standards of morality. They do this in an attempt to sway others in order to rule over them. One such person stated, "We inspire to corrupt in order to rule."[6]

> "Our civilization… can be saved only
> by becoming permeated with the Spirit of Christ."

> "If the Spirit of God is not in us…
> if we will not prepare to give all we have…
> to preserve Christian civilization,
> we shall go to destruction."

How can the people of a nation maintain the moral stability of biblical Christian principles in society? Well, God stands ready to help them do so if those people will turn to Him in prayer.[7] But the bottom line is this, it's up to the people of that nation to get the process started. And not just the general population, but a specific subset of the population. Specifically, those who claim to be called by His name: Christ-ians.[8]

Journal - Personal notes, prayer points, & Scriptures you apply to this lesson.

Question: How does 2 Chronicles 7:14 work in conjunction with 1 Peter 2:9-10? How are Christians to act as a subset of the population in every nation?

60 Days Praying for America

DAY 2

CINO's and the Veneer Problem

> "The moral principles and precepts contained in the Scriptures ought to form the basis of all our civil constitutions and laws. All the miseries and evils which men suffer from - vice, crime, ambition, injustice, oppression, slavery, and war - proceed from the despising or neglecting the precepts contained in the Bible."[1]

EVERY NATION HAS A GOD. If we kick out the God of the Bible, there are dozens of other gods waiting in the darkness for their chance to rush in and fill the void.

> A bill becomes unconstitutional, even though the wording may be constitutionally acceptable, if the legislator who introduced the bill had a religious activity in mind when he authorized it.[2]

And so, the other gods have rushed in. We had no idea judges could read minds and know what legislators were thinking when they introduce a bill. They must be getting help from some of these lesser gods.

There are RINOs and DINOs. Is there such a thing as a CINO - Christian In Name Only? Apparently so. Otherwise, there would only be the Nine Commandments instead of Ten. God would have left out the one that says, *You shall not take the name of the LORD your God in vain, for the LORD will not hold him guiltless who takes His name in vain.*[3] Of course, this has nothing to do with our use of vocabulary. It has everything to do with how we represent the One whose name we bear – 'Christ-ones', or more commonly 'Christ-ians.'

When Jesus talks about those who are called by His name being 'the salt of the earth', 'the light of the world' and a 'city set on a hill'[4], He was talking about the way we should influence secular society with God's Truth. He was talking about those who are called by His name being 'in the world, not of the world.'[5]

There are too many who lay claim to the name 'Christ-ones', but who are nothing more than mere vanity Christians, Christians who have only a thin veneer of being Christ-like. They are more 'of the world' than they are 'transformed into His image.' 'Christian witches' (an oxymoron, if ever there was one) who have been in news headlines lately, come to mind.

Judges can make all the foolish court decisions they like. As true Christians, our response should be, *Whether it is right in the sight of God to listen to you more than God, you judge. For we cannot but speak the things which we have seen and heard.*[6] In other words, your judicial decisions do not overrule the Word of God, your judicial decisions are overruled by the Word of God.

Now is the time for true Christ-ones to pray for our nation and for each other.

Journal - Personal notes, prayer points, & Scriptures you apply to this lesson.

Question: What do Romans 12:1-2, 2 Corinthians 3:18, and Matthew 16:24-25 tell us about being true Christ-ones and not CINOs?

_____

_____

_____

_____

60 Days Praying for America

DAY 3

Turning America Upside-Down!

> "It is in the man of piety and inward principle that we may expect to find the uncorrupted patriot, the useful citizen, and the invincible soldier. God grant that in America true religion and civil liberty may be inseparable and that the unjust attempts to destroy the one, may in the issue tend to the support and establishment of both."[1]

"THAT IN AMERICA TRUE RELIGION (Christianity) and civil liberty may be inseparable…"

Actually, God has already granted that request. In fact, the request needn't even be made. God has already established that principle in His Word.[2] If a people or a nation desire civil liberty let them pursue God and the biblical principles of Christianity.

"That unjust attempts to destroy the one, may in the issue tend to the support and establishment of both."

In other words, any attack on civil liberties should result in the increased strengthening of the biblical principles of Christianity as well as the principles of civil liberties. If you strengthen one, you strengthen the other. Why? Because civil liberty is inseparable from the principles of Christianity.

The problem America faces as a nation today is that the unjust attacks on biblical Christian principles have, in fact, eroded away the basis of our government and therefore our civil liberties. All this occurs even though nearly seventy percent of the populace claim to approve of Christianity. The combined removal of the principles of Christianity and of our civil liberties occurs, not because the attacks of the minority on those who oppose God and the Bible are so effective, but because those who claim to be Christian sit idly by while the attacks take place. They have taken the name of Christ, Christian, needlessly and uselessly. They are mere vanity Christians (CINO: Christian In Name Only!)[3]

Too many of today's Christians sit idly by in the face of relentless attacks by those opposing the One they call Lord. They are too busy being entertained by the world to take time to denounce the attacks, pray for one another, and for the nation.

To be holy is to separate one's self from anything that would keep you from pursuing God (you know, like TV, social media, sports and entertainments, relationships that pull in the wrong direction…) God's call to *you*, Christian, is to *be holy in all your conduct, because it is written, "Be holy, for I am holy.*[4]

Many are unwilling to be holy because it demands a price. Just remember, you get what you pay for! There is a cost to standing idly by while enemies make "unjust attempts to destroy" Christianity in America. The cost is the loss of the liberties and freedoms our forefathers fought for.

The response of the early church, when facing the same opposition we face today (and which comes from the same source[5]), was twofold. First, they prayed. Prayer is our most powerful resource and force. *The effective, fervent prayer of a righteous man avails much!*[6] Second, they spoke the Truth of God's Word boldly. They didn't sit idly by and whine and complain about how bad things were going and how tough things were. They stood up, proclaimed the truth - with all outspokenness, with frankness, publicly, and in entire confidence.[7] And they turned the world upside down!

60 Days Praying for America

Those disciples were willing to *deny themselves, take up their cross and follow Jesus.*[8] It's time to turn America upside down. Are you willing to pay the price to be a true patriot?

Journal - Personal notes, prayer points, & Scriptures you apply to this lesson.

Question: How can you personally apply Mark 8:38 and John 17:14-18 in regards to compromising with the world rather than being 'in the world, not of the world?'

_____

_____

_____

_____

_____

_____

_____

_____

_____

_____

_____

_____

DAY 4

The Hand That Feeds You

> "If you love wealth greater than liberty, the tranquility of servitude greater than the animating conquest for freedom, go home from us in peace. We seek not your counsel, nor your arms. Crouch down and lick the hand that feeds you; and may posterity forget that you were our countrymen."[1]

INCREASE THE HAPPINESS of the general population. Reduce greed and corruption. Share equal profits among everyone. It's the next great, new economic system. Except it isn't new at all, and it's not that great. Throughout history, it's been tried and found to fail again and again. It's called socialism. Whatever is produced by individual citizens is shared equally among all in the community.

"The Tranquility of Servitude"

The first settlers in Jamestown tried socialism. It didn't work. What they discovered was that socialism results in a substandard performance by all those involved. No matter what level of work each of the settlers performed – excellent, mediocre, or none, everyone received the same amount of food and produce. If your hunger pangs increased, it did you no good to give more diligence and effort to your work. You would not receive a greater amount of food to reduce those hunger pangs. If the portion you receive is the same as all the other laborers, why make any extra effort?

In fact, since the diligent and the idle both receive the same portion, why work at all? Socialism is the greatest economic engine that can be found in mankind for generating frivolous and unproductive idlers. The biographers of John Smith, governor of Jamestown, recorded his solution to the problems caused by socialism:

"The majority of them, unaccustomed to discipline or regular employment, showed symptoms of stubborn resistance to his authority, which provoked him to reprove them in sharp terms. He told them that their recent suffering (the 'Starving Time' in which only 60 of 214 settlers survived the winter of 1609) ought to have worked a change in their conduct and that… the majority of them must be industrious or starve – that it was not reasonable that the labors of thirty or forty honest and industrious men should be devoted to the support of a hundred and fifty idle loiterers, and that therefore whoever <u>would</u> not work <u>must</u> not eat."[2]

Oh! Wait! That's a biblical principle! *For even when we were with you, we commanded you this: If anyone will not work, neither shall he eat.*[3]

"Crouch Down and Lick the Hand That Feeds You"

Why then, is the effort to move to an economic system of socialism increasing? Well, for one thing, humans are intrinsically lazy! Laziness is a common character trait found among us all, and it is exacerbated by socialism. But the bottom line reason is this, biblical education has been removed from the nation's schools *and even from the churches*!

A free-market economy places the responsibility to produce directly on the shoulders of the individual. If you want to eat well, prosper, and increase, you're the one who must do the work. The individual cannot leech off the efforts of another. Taking the resources and increase one person works hard to earn and giving them to another person – socialism - is called thievery.

The Founding Fathers got it right: "[A free market is] the means, under God, of recovering and establishing the freedom of our country entire, and of handing it down to posterity."[4] Socialism is the means of enslaving our

60 Days Praying for America

country entire, of inducing citizens to crouch down and lick the hand of government.

Journal - Personal notes, prayer points, & Scriptures you apply to this lesson.

Question: How do Proverbs 10:2-5; 13:4 and Colossians 3:7-8 apply to the economics of socialism?

_____

_____

_____

_____

_____

_____

_____

_____

_____

_____

_____

60 Days Praying for America

DAY 5

A Second Revolution

> "You are putting God before the laws of man. That's not what we do in this country. That's not how it works. Our rights do not come from God... that's not our country. Our laws come from collective agreement and compromise."[1]

> "The Founding Fathers... recognizing God as the author of individual rights, declared that the purpose of Government is to secure those rights... But in many lands the State claims to be the author of human rights. If the State gives rights, it can - and inevitably will - take away those rights. Without God, there could be no American form of Government, nor an American way of life. Recognition of the Supreme Being is the first - the most basic – expression of Americanism. Thus the Founding Fathers saw it, and thus, with God's help, it will continue to be."[2]

A PROBLEM EMERGES from the first comment above: officials, once elected to office, can make whatever laws they want as long as they claim to have discussed the options among themselves. Elected officials can pass laws with no regard for the desires of those who elected them to office. They don't really represent their constituents; they rule over their constituents. That's tyranny. That's why representatives are often heard making comments about how they hold their constituents in such low esteem. We'll refute the person making the first quote with his own words: "That's not what we do in this country. That's not how it works."

The person making the second quote got it right. The framework which governs our nation is what the Founding Fathers referred to as 'Moral Law', the 'laws of nature and of nature's God.' There is a law higher than that of elected officials. There is a law which holds a nation's citizens, government, and elected officials accountable to a higher Law Giver. Without that Law Giver and His law, those we elect to office cease to represent us and instead become our rulers. Such is the case in America today.

The Law Giver referred to by the Founding Fathers is the God of the Bible, not some other imposter, and most certainly not man. The Moral Law which comes from the Law Giver sets out 'inalienable rights', those rights which cannot be denied, taken away, or transferred to another person or entity. The primary purpose of the government established by our Founding Fathers is to secure those inalienable rights, which include the rights to life, liberty, freedom of religion, self-defense, property ownership, home security, secure national borders, and so forth. All of which are outlined in the documents of our nation.

To refute, and rebuke, the first speaker above:

Yes, we are putting God above man and above the laws of man. That's what we do in this country. Our rights come from God, that's our country. Our laws and the inalienable rights they protect come from the Supreme Law Giver and His law, not from the deliberations and compromises of mere men.

Of course, this kind of government and the inalienable rights it secures, can only be preserved when people know and understand biblical principles of righteousness and morality. It can only be preserved when people who understand these principles elect to office those men and women who also abide by and hold themselves accountable to those same principles.

60 Days Praying for America

It is time for a second revolution in America. A revolution where all individual citizens take the personal responsibility to instill in themselves a firm understanding of the pure principles of Christianity and the law of God, and to demand the same from those they elect to office.

"Our citizens should early understand that the genuine source of correct republican principles is the Bible."[3]

Until such a second revolution takes place and we re-gain the understanding of those principles, the government that secures our liberties disintegrates. Then what will become of those liberties?

Journal - Personal notes, prayer points, & Scriptures you apply to this lesson.

Question: Does Luke 10:27 have anything to say about compromise? Does 'love your neighbor as yourself' ever take priority over 'you shall love the Lord your God with all your heart?'

_____

_____

_____

_____

_____

_____

60 Days Praying for America

DAY 6

Fools & Folly: A Shot In the Foot

> "Stupidity is a more dangerous enemy of the good than malice. One may protest against evil; it can be exposed and, if need be, prevented by use of force. Evil always carries within itself the germ of its own subversion in that it leaves behind in human beings at least a sense of unease. Against stupidity we are defenseless. Neither protests nor the use of force accomplish anything here; reasons fall on deaf ears; facts that contradict one's prejudgment simply need not be believed - in such moments the stupid person even becomes critical - and when facts are irrefutable, they are just pushed aside as inconsequential, as incidental. In all this the stupid person, in contrast to the malicious one, is utterly self-satisfied and, being easily irritated, becomes dangerous by going on the attack. For that reason, greater caution is called for when dealing with a stupid person than with a malicious one. Never again will we try to persuade the stupid person with reasons, for it is senseless and dangerous."[1]

IT'S A JUDGMENT CALL you have to make when dealing with a fool. *Do not answer a fool according to his folly, lest you also be like him. Answer a fool according to his folly, lest he be wise in his own eyes.*[2] Some fools don't deserve a response, so it's best to ignore them so you don't end up like them. Or, you can make it a matter of record that the fool is wrong if it appears there is hope for his correction. How to respond to a fool is a tough call to make.

Only a fool would say there is no God.[3] Only a fool would place themselves on the wrong side of an issue in opposition to God. Yet that is what many politicians, judges, educators, and the John and Jane Q. Public's have done in America. What could be the cause of such foolishness? Ignorance? Well, yes, that could be the cause. Nearly sixty years ago there were fools in America that eliminated teaching the Bible, the Ten Commandments, and prayer from the education system. So, today's fools could claim ignorance due to a lack of a proper education. Regretfully, many church leaders became fools as well, failing to pick up the slack. They also failed in teaching the Bible's principles of morality. Talk about shooting yourself in the foot!

America's Founding Fathers were no fools. They had a firm grasp on the understanding that whatever might make a person an enemy of God would equally cripple the moral character of society and thus would have the same pernicious effect on the nation as a whole. Because of their strong convictions on Christianity, America's Founders were quick to respond to any attack against the principles of Christian righteousness. They knew that the security of our nation relied entirely on this "indispensable support."[4]

Professing to be wise, some of today's Americans have become fools; they have set themselves in direct opposition to God, His law, and His standard of righteousness. The aforementioned deleterious effects on society and the nation can be readily observed, just read and listen to the news.

There are two things that can be done to turn the tide. First, those who truly desire the principles of Christian righteousness to be restored in America can humble themselves before God, pray, and repent (change what needs changing in your life). Remember, *God resists the proud, but gives grace to the humble. Draw near to God and He will draw near to you.*[5]

Second, ask God to raise up bold-as-a-lion preachers of righteousness. *The wicked flee when no one pursues, but the righteous are bold as a lion.*[6]

Why should we be bold in preaching, teaching, and declaring the Word of God? Because *all Scripture is God-breathed and is profitable for*

60 Days Praying for America

- *Doctrine:* which tells us what is right.
- *Reproof:* which tells us what is not right.
- *Correction:* which tells us how to get it right.
- *Instruction:* which tells us how to keep it right.[7]

If we do these things, there may be hope for fools and for America itself.

Journal - Personal notes, prayer points, & Scriptures you apply to this lesson.

Question: Using Psalms 119:125-128 and Matthew 28:18-20, and understanding that our government, judges, and some churches fail to stand for righteousness, where does the responsibility for holding a standard of righteousness now lay?

_____

_____

_____

_____

_____

_____

_____

_____

_____

_____

DAY 7

An Easy Lesson

> "Reason and experience both forbid us to expect that national morality can prevail in exclusion of religious principle. If we work upon marble, it will perish. If we work upon brass, time will efface it. If we rear temples, they will crumble to dust. But, if we work upon immortal minds, and instill into them just principles, we are then engraving upon that tablet that which no time will efface, but will brighten and brighten to all eternity. If we abide by the principles taught in the Bible, our country will go on prospering and to prosper; but if we and our posterity neglect its instructions and authority, no man can tell how sudden a catastrophe may overwhelm us and bury all our glory in profound obscurity."[1]

WHAT'S GOOD FOR THE GOOSE is good for the gander. If America expects its citizens to behave with moral character, then the government must also. George Washington affirmed this understanding when he publicly stated the four duties that govern every nation:

"It is the duty of <u>all</u> nations to:

1. Acknowledge the providence of Almighty God (recognize and profess His guidance in the affairs of the nation),
2. Obey His will,
3. Be grateful for His benefits (express thankfulness for His assistance and prosperity),
4. Humbly implore His protection and favor. (Pray!)."[2]

60 Days Praying for America

Armed with the knowledge that no republican form of government can stand firm nor can it secure the liberties and freedoms of its people unless the people themselves have a moral character firmly rooted in biblical Christian principles, the Founding Fathers of America made every effort and provision to see to it that those same principles were supported and taught both in all the churches of America and in the nation's system of public education.

Unfortunately, over time our nation's leaders forsook this understanding and relinquished any support of churches and schools in the teaching of biblical righteousness. With no further support of the government or the judicial system, the responsibility fell upon the churches and church leaders themselves. However, too many of those no longer preach and teach righteousness, but rather a 'social gospel' and a 'tolerance gospel.'

Jesus never said, "The gates of hades shall not prevail against the Church." What He said was this: *On this Rock I will build My church, and the gates of Hades will not prevail against it.*[3] The "it" Jesus refers to is not the "church", but the "Rock." What Jesus was saying is this, *"On this Rock I will build My church and the gates of Hades shall not prevail against the Rock, nor against the church founded upon the Rock."*[3] This implies that not all churches are built upon the Rock, and therefore, the gates of Hades *will prevail* against a church that is not built on the Rock. Evidence of that can be seen in America today.

In view of this situation, the question becomes two-fold. First, what is the "Rock"? The "Rock" is the revelation that Peter received from God, the revelation that "Jesus is the Christ". Jesus is the only One who can provide any means of salvation and lead a person or a nation to God.[4]

Second, how does a church "build upon the Rock?" Jesus again answered that question with His statement that *whoever hears these sayings of Mine, and does them, I will liken him to a wise man who built his house on the Rock… everyone who hears these sayings of Mine, and does not do them, will be like a foolish man who built his house on the sand…*[5] Both a person and a nation are built on the Rock by <u>hearing</u> and <u>doing</u> the Word of God. It's an easy lesson to understand and integrate.

The Founding Fathers were building on the Rock. Unfortunately, for some time now the leaders of America's government and judicial system along with several of its citizens have become quite foolish. They have been building on the sand, regarding and breaking God's law as void, suppressing the truth in unrighteousness, and devising evil by law.[6]

When our government and judicial systems abandon building on the Rock, it becomes incumbent upon the American people to truly seek God by

1. acknowledging the providence of Almighty God,
2. obeying His will,
3. expressing gratitude for His benefits, and
4. humbly imploring His protection and favor. Pray!

"If we abide by the principles taught in the Bible, our country will go on prospering and to prosper; but if we and our posterity neglect its instructions and authority…"

Journal - Personal notes, prayer points, & Scriptures you apply to this lesson.

Question: Consider Psalms 43:3; 119:130; and John 1:4-5: how would you apply those in prayer to this lesson?

_____

_____

_____

_____

60 Days Praying for America

DAY 8

Primary Voter Problems

> "It is a great mistake to suppose that the paper we are to propose (the Constitution) will govern the United States. It is the men whom it will bring into the government and interest they have in maintaining it, that are to govern them. The paper will only mark out the mode and the form. Men are the substance and must do the business."[1]

THE PRIMARY PROBLEM AMERICA FACES today is a spiritual problem. America's problem is not the government, it's spiritual! America's primary problem is not politics, it's spiritual. It's not the left, it's spiritual. It's not the right, it's spiritual. The problem's not civil rights, it's spiritual. America's problem is not homosexual rights, it's a spiritual problem. It's not the economy (stupid!), it's spiritual. It's not borders or anything else on your list of complaints. It's spiritual!

Because the real problem in America is spiritual, the solution to the problem lies in the hearts of all people. So often prayers are made asking God for this bill to pass or that resolution to fail. We pray for this particular person in that particular office. We pray for abortion to end and the economy to improve. Those are issues that need prayer. But those are only symptoms of the root problem.

"Men are the substance and must do the business."

The Constitution is a piece of paper that gives America's citizens the authority to elect leaders who will govern on their behalf. The system of law established at America's founding is good. But if unscrupulous and weak people are voted into office they may, and will, ignore the Constitution and its founding principles. As computer programmers say, 'Garbage in, garbage out.' As the Bible puts it, *When the righteous are in authority, the people rejoice; but when a wicked man rules, the people groan.*[2]

It is then, in the midst of all their groaning that voters clamor for new leadership. Voters need to understand that sound government doesn't depend on the Constitution and laws, but on how good our leaders are. How good our leaders are, depends on how good the voters themselves are. The condition of America's culture and government is a reflection of the spiritual condition in the hearts of the voters - and non-voters.

> "There must be religion [the Christian religion, not others]. When that ligament is torn, society is disjointed and its members perish. The nation is exposed to foreign violence and domestic convulsion. Vicious [ungodly] rulers chosen by vicious [ungodly] people, turn back the current of corruption to its source. Placed in a situation where they can execute authority for their own endowment, they betray their trust. They take bribes. They sell statutes and decrees. They sell honor and office. They sell their conscience. They sell their country… But the most important of all lessons is the denunciation of ruin to every State that rejects the precepts of [the Christian] religion."[3]

The primary problem America faces today is a spiritual problem. That spiritual problem resides in the heart of voters in America. The cure to that spiritual problem lies in restoring the biblical principles of Christianity – righteousness – in the heart of the voters. Neither America's government nor America as a nation can or will survive if righteousness is not found in the hearts of its people. Praying for the issues is okay. However, the most pressing need is praying for those who vote, and for those who are negligent in that trust.

60 Days Praying for America

Journal - Personal notes, prayer points, & Scriptures you apply to this lesson.

Question: Considering Proverbs 29:2; 28:12; and Matt. 28:18: can a 'leader' (or even you!) "Go" in any sense of the command if they are not properly authorized? Under who's authority should our leaders – and you - be operating?

_____

_____

_____

_____

_____

_____

_____

_____

_____

_____

_____

_____

_____

_____

DAY 9

Got Apples?

> "The free, equal, and undisturbed, enjoyment of religious opinion ... is granted... But to revile, with malicious and blasphemous contempt, the religion professed by almost the whole community, is an abuse of that right. Nor are we bound ... to punish indiscriminately the like attacks upon the religion of Mahomet or of the grand Lama ... for this plain reason ... that we are a Christian people, and the morality of the country is deeply ingrafted upon Christianity, and not upon the doctrines or worship of those impostors ..."[1]

"... WE ARE A CHRISTIAN PEOPLE, and the morality of the country is deeply ingrafted upon Christianity, and not upon the doctrines or worship of those impostors."

CoeXisT. Social cohesion through education, including being inculcated with the idea that all religions are equal and serve the same God. Or, that people should all be allowed to worship whatever god they want just as long as they don't bother other people. Here's some real education on the topic of CoeXisT.

Apple trees will always produce apples. Pear trees will always produce pears. Strawberry plants will always produce strawberries. And potato plants will always produce potatoes.

Not only is the morality of America deeply ingrafted upon the principles of Christianity, but the liberties of America are secured by those same principles.

60 Days Praying for America

The more the people of America adhere to the biblical principalities of Christianity, the more secure will be our form of government and our liberties.

Apple trees will always produce apples. This is a principle of life. If you want apples, you've got to plant apple seeds. You won't get apples from a pear seed. The fruit produced by following the principles of Christianity will always produce liberty. Liberty in America will never be produced by following the doctrines of any other religion. The principles of morality laid out in the Bible are very clear. The Bible also makes clear the consequences of disobeying and the benefits – the liberties – found in obeying those principles.

Over centuries, the Bible's prohibitions against and encouragement of certain types of behaviors have never changed nor altered. God states very clearly what the fruit of living in disobedience to His Word will be. He also clearly states what fruit is produced by obedience to His will. The instruction of other religions will never produce the same fruit – the liberties – as will the instruction found in the Christian Bible. America's Founding Fathers were adamant about this, not just on several occasions, but constantly.

Jesus said, *If you abide in My word, you are My disciples indeed. And you shall know the truth, and the truth shall make you free.*[2] It is the truth you know and obey that will make you free – that will give you liberty.

Trees are judged by their fruit. *A good tree does not bear bad fruit, nor does a bad tree bear good fruit. For every tree is known by its own fruit. For men do not gather figs from thorns, nor do they gather grapes from a bramble bush. A good man out of the good treasure of his heart brings forth good; and an evil man out of the evil treasure of his heart brings forth evil. For out of the abundance of the heart his mouth speaks.*[3]

America does not have a political problem. America has a morality problem. Out of the abundance of the heart, we bring forth bondage or we bring forth liberty. Out of the abundance of our heart, we produce servitude or we produce liberty.

You can't get apples by planting pear seeds.

Journal - Personal notes, prayer points, & Scriptures you apply to this lesson.

Question: Considering 2 Corinthians 10:4-6, what arguments and high things has the Word of God been subjugated to in America? What strongholds have Americans put more trust in than the God of the Bible? What are the weapons listed in Hebrews 4:12-13; Revelation 12:11; and Mark 16:17 that Christians are to use for pulling down these strongholds?

_____

_____

_____

_____

_____

_____

_____

_____

_____

_____

DAY 10

Manners & Self-Government

> "Our government rests upon religion. It is from that source that we derive our reverence for truth and justice, for equality and liberty, and for the rights of mankind. Unless the people believe in these principles they cannot believe in our government. Calling the people to righteousness is a direct preparation for self-government.
>
> The ability for self-government is arrived at only through an extensive training and education. It is of a great deal of significance that the generation which fought the American Revolution had seen a very extensive religious revival. They had heard the preaching of Jonathan Edwards. They had seen the great revival meetings that were inspired also by the preaching of George Whitefield.
>
> The religious experiences of those days made a profound impression upon the great body of the people. They freed the public mind through a deeper knowledge and more serious contemplation of the truth. By calling the people to righteousness they were a direct preparation for self-government. We cannot depend on the government to do the work of religion. We cannot escape a personal responsibility for our own conduct. We cannot regard those as wise or safe counselors in public affairs who deny these principles..."[1]

AMERICA'S FORM OF GOVERNMENT was created to secure the freedom and liberties of individuals. It was not created to allow individual licentiousness. If a government is to secure the individual's freedom and liberty, it must also provide the individual with a means for self-government, a means for the individual to control himself without the need for the government to control him. An individual who cannot control himself will require the force of the law to bring him under control.

Therefore, from the outset, the means of self-government the Founding Fathers insisted be provided to the individual was a call to righteousness. Specifically, a call for the individual to live by the standards of righteousness found in the Christian Bible.

> **"The ability for self-government is arrived at only through an extensive training and education."**

The individual cannot be manipulated or coerced into believing and following biblical principles of righteousness. Nevertheless, those principles can and should be extended to all individuals. They can and should be modeled and taught to every person. It will then be the responsibility of the individual to accept and live by those principles of righteousness, or to reject them. The individual has a free conscience in this regard. Should the individual choose to reject those standards, the Founders established laws that would provide boundaries for the actions of that individual. The individual would no longer be self-governed, but would be ruled by an external authority.

> **We cannot depend on the government to do the work of religion. We cannot escape a personal responsibility for our own conduct.**

For far too many decades now, our 'leaders' have been forcefully removing prayer, the Bible, and the teaching of Christian standards of righteousness from of America's educational process, and from government, society, and culture. In place of the Christian religion they substitute secular humanism, the government will take over the work of religion. Today, because the individual lacks righteousness and is incapable of self-government, legislators pass more and more laws to control the individual. It will not be long before tyranny and a tyrant step in to gain complete control. Then liberty and freedom will be lost.

**We cannot regard those as wise or safe
counselors in public affairs who deny these principles…**

"Those who will not be ruled by God, will be ruled by tyrants."[2]

Journal - Personal notes, prayer points, & Scriptures you apply to this lesson.

Question: Where did Jesus say the Kingdom of God is to be found? (hint: Luke 17:21) Who is the ruler of your life, you or Jesus? Read Mark 7:20-23 How well are you ruling what's in your heart? How do Proverbs 16:32; 25:28 and 1 Corinthians 9:25 apply to this lesson?

_____

_____

_____

_____

_____

_____

_____

_____

_____

_____

_____

DAY 11

Kiss and Make Up

> "To the kindly influence of Christianity, we owe that degree of civil freedom and political and social happiness which mankind now enjoy. In proportion as the genuine effects of Christianity are diminished in any nation… in the same proportion will the people of that nation recede from the blessings of genuine freedom… All efforts made to destroy the foundations of our Holy Religion ultimately tend to the subversion of our political freedom and happiness. Whenever the pillars of Christianity shall be overthrown, our present republican forms of government – and all the blessings which flow from them – must fall with them."[1]

JESUS WAS THE MOST ANTI-RELIGIOUS MAN to ever walk the face of the earth. Religion is nothing more than man's attempt to "kiss and make up" with God. Religion is mankind's attempt to do good works in an effort to convince God that we're not so bad after all. The problem with this approach is that there are not enough good works, nor is there any one good work we can do that will impress God to the point of restoring our relationship with Him. No one can appease God's standards of righteousness through good works.

Mankind's biggest challenge is not that we are basically good but occasionally do bad things. Our true problem is that we are inherently bad and only occasionally will we do good. Have you ever noticed that you don't have to train children to behave badly? They do 'bad' all by themselves.

60 Days Praying for America

What parents have to do is train them to be good. Why is this? Because all children are born with a sin nature.

God fully understood that all of us were all completely incapable of resolving this relationship problem by ourselves. The attempt to restore mankind's relationship with God depends entirely on His initiative, not ours. Jesus' primary purpose in coming to earth was to restore man's relationship with God. At no time did He ever indicate that this could be accomplished through good works. The only way Jesus was able to restore our relationship with God was through His death on the Cross followed by His burial and resurrection.

Jesus made this perfectly clear when He said, *I am the way, the truth, and the life. <u>No one</u> comes to the Father except through Me.*[2] When it comes to knowing God, Jesus is not just one option in a pantheon of gods. He's the only option!

How does this apply to a nation, to praying for a nation? Quite simply, America's liberties come from God. Not from man, nor from the government. When we abandon God and His principles of righteousness, our liberties, "and all the blessings which flow from them", erode away. It's not hard to see this erosion of liberties taking place today. Just read the news headlines and listen to the babble of political candidates.

And while you're listening to that babble, listen to the babble of the politically correct pulpits across America. Preaching moral compromise with pop culture and social justice warriors, they fail to uphold God's standards of righteousness. Too many are taught from the pulpit that "God helps those who help themselves."

Sorry, no. Jesus did not die on the cross to get you a new house and a new spouse. He didn't die on the cross to get you a new car and make you a star. The Holy Spirit is not a symbol of God's power, He is God Himself. Satan is real. And as stated previously, there are not many paths to God, just one – Jesus Christ.

It is time for Christians to pray for the truth of God's Word to be proclaimed: *All things that are exposed are made manifest by the light, for whatever makes manifest is light. The entrance of Your Word gives light; it gives understanding to the simple.* It is time for people in America to truly "get woke!" *Therefore, Lord, You say: 'Awake, you who sleep, arise from the dead, and Christ will give you light.'*[3]

If we want to restore and safeguard America's liberties, it's time to kiss and make up with God: *Now therefore, be wise, O kings; be instructed, you judges of the earth. Serve the LORD with fear, and rejoice with trembling. Kiss the Son, lest He be angry, and you perish in the way, when His wrath is kindled but a little. Blessed are all those who put their trust in Him.*[4]

Journal - Personal notes, prayer points, & Scriptures you apply to this lesson.

Question: Romans 12:2 calls us to live by God's standards, not the world's standards. 1 John 2:15-17 gives an even sterner warning. Compare these two verses with 1 John 4:4. As Christians, what should our respective attitudes be towards Jesus Christ?

_____

_____

_____

_____

_____

_____

60 Days Praying for America

DAY 12

America's Heart Problem

> "A humanities course currently taught at the University of Colorado Springs teaches that the Founding Fathers were hypocrites, terrorists and money-hungry barons who used hyperbole and fear to rile up the colonists to revolt against England."[1]

> "The education of the youth should be watched with the most scrupulous attention. Education forms the moral characters of men, and morals are the basis of government. Education should therefore be the first care of political regulations; for it is much easier to introduce and establish an effectual system for preserving morals than to correct by penal statutes the ill effects of a bad system. The goodness of the heart is of infinitely more consequence than an elegance of manners. The education of the youth lays the foundation on which both law and gospel rest for success."[2]

THE SUPPORTING STRUCTURE OF GOVERNMENT is the morals of men. The morals of men are formed by education. Therefore, the "education of the youth should be watched with the most scrupulous attention."

Some time ago people with far less wisdom than America's Founding Fathers decided that the thing to do would be to remove Bible reading, prayer and the Ten Commandments from education. They removed the most "effectual system for preserving morals" from the educational system, and thereby removed the supporting structure of our government. Genius.

60 Days Praying for America

*The fear of the LORD is the beginning of knowledge,
but fools despise wisdom and instruction.*[3]

What are some of the results of these uneducated court judgments?

According to a study by the Educational Testing Service, there are only two countries with a literary proficiency worse than American Millennials. And America's Millennials are dead last in math.[4]

Here are a few more statistics proving "it is much easier to introduce and establish an effectual system for preserving morals than to correct by penal statutes the ill effects of a bad system."[5]

- Lack a high school education… That's okay, if you're a criminal they'll pay you $1000 a month not to shoot people.[6]
- The highest-paid public employee in more than half the states is a football coach.[7]
- Not many people read books anymore (even if they know how to read), yet the average American spends just over 5 hours a day watching television.[8]
- Seventy-five percent of young adults cannot find Iraq on a map of the Middle East, but they sure know how to find porn on the Internet.[9]
- There are more than 4 million adult websites on the Internet today, and they get more traffic than Netflix, Amazon and Twitter combined.[10]

America's education system is in shambles. It has little to do with real education, and everything to do with operating a money mill for those who run the system. And now there is the talk of 'free education' for everyone, thus guarantying the grubbers running the mill of making even more money from taxpayers.

Take firm hold of instruction, do not let go; keep her, for she is your life.[11]

Our Founding Fathers knew the importance of *taking firm hold of instruction*. It is time for true Christians to pray and seek God until America's education

60 Days Praying for America

system is repaired and restored to its original purpose. It is time to take firm hold of God in prayer until He takes firm hold of our educational system, restoring His Word, His commandments, and prayer to restore moral character in students, and thus a firm basis for America's government.

Journal - Personal notes, prayer points, & Scriptures you apply to this lesson.

Question: Proverbs 4:13 is a command. How would you obey it, and what would be required for you to achieve this command? For your children to achieve this command?

_____

_____

_____

_____

_____

_____

_____

_____

_____

_____

_____

_____

_____

DAY 13

Separation & Restitution

> "We're a nation under God, a living and loving God. But Thomas Jefferson warned us, 'Indeed, I tremble for my country when I reflect that God is just: that his justice cannot sleep forever…' We cannot expect Him to protect us in crisis if we turn away from Him in our everyday living."[1]

WILL GOD JUDGE AMERICA? One response to that question was a quip made by Billy Graham, 'If God doesn't judge America, He'll have to apologize to Sodom and Gomorrah.'

Most people misunderstand the purpose of God's judgment. They view it as a punishment resulting in total destruction. From a biblical perspective, this is not so. The term judgment means 'to separate.' I don't like red M&M's. If I open a package of M&M's and toss out all the red ones and eat the rest, I have judged the red M&M's. I separated out the red ones. When God judges a person, organization, or nation His purpose is to remove – to separate out – what is bad from what is good according to His standards. What makes that judgment seem so hard to some people is that their desire is for the bad, not for the good.

The second purpose in God's judgments is redemption. He separates out what is evil so He can restore His order, His good. The main goal of all God's judgments is redemption, restoring His order and His righteousness in the life of a person, an organization, or a nation. God's judgments are not for punishment, they are to produce redemption, they are a form of discipline to encourage us to follow after His order, to seek His holiness.

> *But judgment will return to righteousness,*
> *and all the upright in heart will follow it.*[2]

God is extremely patient. He will give warning after warning to stop doing what will ultimately end in destruction. However, after a period of time, God ceases His warning and lets people and nations continue on to the logical yet destructive end of their thoughts and actions.

> *The nations have sunk down in the pit which they made;*
> *in the net which they hid, their own foot is caught.*
> *The LORD is known by the judgment He executes;*
> *the wicked is snared in the work of his own hands.*[3]

Will God judge America? Barring a nationwide revival and return to His standards of righteousness and holiness, ultimately, He will have to. Our 'leaders, all of whom *we* voted into office, have done everything they can to remove God, His Word, and His law from as many aspects of our society as possible. America is the worldwide leader in the distribution of pornography – the exploitation of children, women, and men for the fulfillment of another person's lust for physical pleasure. America is also the worldwide leader in promoting child sacrifice - the killing of innocent, unborn children, more commonly referred to as abortion. Abortion has now been advanced (and regrettably joyously celebrated) to the level of infanticide – killing babies after they are born merely because they are considered an inconvenience.

Will God's judgment of America wash away the filth of evil from our land and society, and restore His righteousness and holiness in our lives? I, for one, believe it will, primarily for two reasons.

First, in spite of strong opposition from some of our 'leaders', America has almost always been a strong supporter of Israel. God's promise has always been to watch over and to bless, those who benefit Israel.

60 Days Praying for America

Second, there are many Christians who are actively praying for our nation. Part of the disconnect here is that some Christians will vote into office 'leaders' who will neither stand for nor support God's biblical standards of righteousness. Abortion is a case in point. Nonetheless, as long as we have those who are praying effectively and sincerely, I believe God will discipline America for the purpose of redeeming us.

The speaker in the opening quote went on to say, "But you know, He told us what to do in 2 Chronicles...He said, *'If my people, which are called by My name, will humble themselves and pray and seek my face and turn from their wicked ways, then I will hear from Heaven and will forgive their sin and will heal their land.'*"

Journal - Personal notes, prayer points, & Scriptures you apply to this lesson.

Question: Considering Matthew 7:1-2, what is the difference between passing judgment on a person or a nation and warning a person or a nation about facing pending judgment?

_____

_____

_____

_____

_____

_____

_____

60 Days Praying for America

DAY 14

Same Heart, Same Mind

> "He is the best friend to American liberty who is most sincere and active in promoting true and undefiled religion, and who sets himself with the greatest firmness to bear down on profanity and immorality of every kind. Whoever is an avowed enemy of God, I scruple not (would have no qualms) to call him an enemy to his country."[1]

DURING THE DAYS OF AMERICA'S FOUNDING FATHERS, Thomas Paine wrote a book entitled *The Age of Reason* in which he vehemently declared his ill will and opposition to Christianity. In the days of America's Founding Fathers, Thomas Paine was a lone voice. When Benjamin Franklin read the booklet, his response was immediate and forcefully against the sentiments Paine expressed:

> "He that spits into the wind, spits into his own face… Think how great a portion of mankind… have need of the motives of religion to restrain them from vice – to support their virtue… I would advise you, therefore, not to attempt unchaining the tiger, but to burn this piece before it is seen by any other person."[2]

Similarly, when U.S Supreme court justice William Paterson was made aware that a handful of citizens agreed with Paine's premise, his response was equally immediate and forceful,

> "Infatuated Americans! Why renounce your country, your religion, and your God? Oh shame, where is thy blush? Is this the way to continue independent and to render the 4th of July immortal in memory and song?"[3]

Infatuated indeed! Far too many American Christians today are infatuated with the comforts brought on by prosperity and safety. They sit at ease, uninvolved, thinking the issues we face are not their problem. Let the leaders we elected handle this. Let the guy in the pulpit handle this. Just let me keep my num-nums. Oh, foolish Americans! Who has beguiled you? For as sure as the Christian religion crumbles away, so too, do your liberties and freedoms crumble away, until all that remains is licentiousness and tyranny.

Paterson equated ill will and opposition against the Christian religion as tantamount to "renouncing your country." John Witherspoon denounced Paine as being "ignorant of human nature as well as an enemy to the Christian faith."[4] And John Quincy Adams stated that "Mr. Paine has departed altogether from the principles of the revolution."[5]

All of the Founding Fathers had the complete understanding that the Christian religion and America's republican form of government were inseparable, they were bound together in principle and in health. To damage one is to damage the other.

In his final years, Thomas Paine was a social outcast. When he passed away no American cemetery would accept his remains, so he was buried in a cow pasture.

One wonders if there are enough cow pastures today…

- A Christian father was arrested in Lexington, MA, for objecting to the public school teaching his kindergarten son about homosexuality and gay marriage.[6]

60 Days Praying for America

- Two Gideons were arrested in Florida for standing on a sidewalk and giving Bibles to those who wanted them.[7]
- A school official in St. Louis, MO, caught an elementary student praying over his lunch; he lifted the student from his seat, reprimanded him in front of the other students, and took him to the principal's office, who ordered him to stop praying.[8] (Talk about bullying!)

The disciples of the early church, facing exactly the same kind of resistance, understood that they *wrestled not against flesh and blood, but against principalities, against powers, against the rulers of the darkness of this age, against spiritual hosts of wickedness in the heavenly places*.[9] So, they did two things. First, they prayed for God's help in working against those tyrannical unseen forces. Second, they could not and would not be stopped from proclaiming the truth of God's Word.

Whether it is right in the sight of God to listen to you more than to God, you judge. For we cannot but speak the things which we have seen and heard.[10]

Our Founding Fathers were of the same heart and mind as those early disciples.

Journal - Personal notes, prayer points, & Scriptures you apply to this lesson.

Question: Matthew 7:21 says it is one thing for a person to say "Jesus is my Lord", but it is entirely another thing for a person to obey Him as Lord. In view of this lesson, which of these persons is "the best friend to American liberty? How does Psalm 71:15-18 apply to living a life as "the best friend to American liberty?

_____

_____

_____

60 Days Praying for America

DAY 15

Polar Opposites

> "Without morals a republic cannot subsist any length of time; they therefore who are decrying the Christian religion, whose morality is so sublime and pure and which insures to the good eternal happiness, are undermining the solid foundation of morals, the best security for the duration of free governments."[1]

AMERICA'S FOUNDING FATHERS confronted the very same issue we face today. They repeatedly used a two-part theme to refute the contentions of some protesters:

1. America's form of government cannot endure any length of time without morals embedded in the hearts and minds of its citizens.
2. The best basis of morals for Americans are the biblical principles of Christianity.

America's government is designed to secure freedom and liberty for all men. Those liberties can only be secure when the same moral principles are applied across the board for all citizens – when everyone is on the same page. Does this mean that everyone must abide by biblical moral principles? No. The Founders also allowed for freedom of conscience. The decision to live by Christian moral principles is up to the individual. Nonetheless, with the goal being the preservation of our government, those are the moral principles that will be applied across the board in America.

60 Days Praying for America

When you observe your civil liberties being degraded and denied, rest assured the reason is due to the decline of Christianity in the land. Slowly but surely, over the last ten or more decades, forces of corruption have eaten away at the broad applications of Christian morality, denying its presence and application in greater and greater degrees. Since nature abhors a vacuum, something must rush in to replace the moral basis of Christianity in America. And indeed, something has filled that empty space.

Moral relativism. What's good for you isn't necessarily what's good for me. Just because it's true for you, doesn't mean it has to be true for me. Rather than truth applied across the board for everyone, truth now varies from person-to-person, place-to-place, circumstance-to-circumstance.

True liberty is freedom of expression under the restrictions of a moral standard, in America's case, the moral standard of Christianity. Licentiousness is merely expressing yourself in whatever manner you please without the restraints of any moral standard. True liberty and licentiousness are polar opposites. In America, true liberty has been exchanged for licentiousness. The basis of moral truth, which was once a solid foundation supporting America's government, has now become a vast unmanageable substrate of shifting sands. As those sands shift, America's form of government crumbles and our liberties sink into the quicksand of dissolution.

If it feels good, do it. Or as the Bible puts it, *everyone was doing what was right in their own eyes*.[2] It was God's indictment against the people of Israel. And it is His indictment against Americans today. People are free to abide by the moral principles of Christianity, or not. But they are not free to remove those principles from American society, culture, or government. To do so is treasonous because it fragments the once-solid foundation of our government. To do so bears the heavy weight of repercussions: *Do you see a man* – or a nation - *wise in his own eyes? There is more hope for a fool than for him.*[3]

60 Days Praying for America

It is time to repair our once sturdy foundation of moral principle. But that is nothing we can do by ourselves. We *must* implore the help of Him whose moral standards we so desperately depend on.

Journal - Personal notes, prayer points, & Scriptures you apply to this lesson.

Question: How would Mark 7:20-23 correspond with today's focus? How well are you personally and America as a whole, supporting our liberties by living a moral life? What could you personally, or America as a whole, do better in this regard?

_____

_____

_____

_____

_____

_____

_____

_____

_____

_____

DAY 16

The Art of Kneeling

> "A patriot without religion, in my estimation, is as great a paradox as an honest man without the fear of God. Is it possible that he whom no moral obligations bind, can have any real good will towards men? Can he be a patriot who, by an openly vicious conduct, is undermining the very bonds of society, corrupting the morals of youth, and by his bad example injuring the very country he professes to patronize more than he can possibly compensate by intrepidity, generosity, and honour?"[1]

ARE CHRISTIANS CALLED to be Republicans or Democrats or Libertarians or just plain old Independents? We are not called to be any of those! We are called to be Monarchists! We are called to be true ambassadors of the Coming King, the Lord Jesus Christ. We are called to stand for the Covenants, Law, and Truth of his Kingdom.

The *manifold wisdom of God is to be made known <u>by the church</u> to the principalities and powers in the heavenlies.*[2] God's purpose is to use the church to deliver the victory He accomplished in the life, death, burial, and resurrection of Jesus Christ throughout the earth – to all nations, including America. And to display that victory before all the powers of evil.

God gave Jeremiah authority over nations, to *root out, to pull down, to destroy, to throw down, to build and to plant.*[3] That sounds very similar to the church's mission statement to display the manifold wisdom of God in every nation, right in front of all the powers of heaven. How did God tell Jeremiah to do this? *Behold, I have put my words in your mouth.* How has God told the church to fulfill its mission? In addition to Matthew 28:20, we are also told that *the effective, fervent prayer of a righteous man avails much.*[4] Many Christians misunderstand the real purpose of prayer. Prayer is not so much for petitions as it is obtaining getting God's direction in fulfilling His purposes. Fervent effectual prayer is praying God's Word according to His will, not our will.

The mystery of lawlessness is already at work... You can observe it in the behavior and conversations of people all around you. It is heard in the news media every day. We are also told that *only He who now restrains will do so until He is taken out of the way.*[5] Too many Christians vote, fuss, cuss, moan, and groan about politics, culture, and society. And they never accomplish a bit of good or the will of God. Why? Because they're vanity Christians. Christians in name only, living just like the world lives and talking just like the world talks.

The weapons of our warfare are not carnal but mighty in God for pulling down strongholds, casting down arguments and every high thing that exalts itself against the knowledge of God, bringing every thought into captivity to the obedience of Christ.[6]

One of those weapons is the Word of God. What is needed is for Christians to get in the Bible, learn God's righteous standards, and to pray according to His Word! Read His Word and ask the Holy Spirit to teach you. Just as soldiers must contact headquarters for direction, He will get His Word in your heart and teach you how to pray accordingly.

For the word of God is living and powerful,
and sharper than any two-edged sword,
piercing even to the division of soul and spirit, and of joints and marrow,
and is a discerner of the thoughts and intents of the heart.
And there is no creature hidden from His sight,

60 Days Praying for America

*but all things are naked and open
to the eyes of Him to whom we must give account.*[7]

Journal - Personal notes, prayer points, & Scriptures you apply to this lesson.

Question: Isaiah 59:17; 2 Corinthians 6:7; and Ephesians 6:14 refer to righteousness in warfare. How will these verses affect the witness of a Christian living a worldly lifestyle and one living a righteous lifestyle? How will it affect their prayer life?

DAY 17

Heart Disease

> "It is sufficient that the common law checks upon words and actions dangerous to the public welfare… whose morals have been elevated and inspired with a more enlarged benevolence, by means of the Christian religion. … the Constitution… does not forbid judicial cognizance of those offenses against religion and morality… punishable because they strike at the root of moral obligation, and weaken the security of the social ties…"[1]

JAMES KENT, along with Joseph Story, was known as the 'Father of American Jurisprudence.' In his day, he was the highest-ranking judicial official in the state of New York. In sixteen years, his courts had only eight murder convictions. Now, why would that be?

America's government was originally established as a Constitutional Republic. All Founding Fathers, including James Kent, had the firm understanding that the ability of a Constitutional Republic to secure liberties and freedoms (not licentiousness) would entirely *'depend upon the piety, religion, and morality'*[2] of its citizens.

The Founding Fathers knew where crimes originate. Not in the external circumstances and environments people face, but in the heart of man. A man is not a car thief because he steals a car. A man steals a car because he is a car thief. You don't have to train your children to behave badly, it is their nature to do so. Bad behavior resides in them from the moment they are born.

60 Days Praying for America

What comes out of a man, that defiles a man.
For from within, out of the heart of men, proceed evil thoughts,
adulteries, fornications, murders, thefts, covetousness, wickedness,
deceit, lewdness, an evil eye, blasphemy, pride, foolishness.
All these evil things come from within and defile a man.[2]

America's Founders took great pains to make sure the biblical principles of the Christian religion were promoted throughout society. They made sure Christianity was promoted in government and in education and in the judiciary. They did this because they knew if people were not controlled by the internal restraints provided through the Bible, the only other option for controlling them was by force.

> "Men, in a word, must necessarily be controlled either by a power within them or a power without them, either by the Word of God or by the strongest arm of man, either by the Bible or by the bayonet."[3]

As America's political and judicial leaders continue to go against the wisdom of the Founding Fathers, increasing prohibitions against Christianity and denying its encouragement, we draw closer to the bayonet. People who vote these leaders into office share the blame. But the bottom line is this, those who call themselves 'Christians' need to quit bowing their knee to their favorite political party, quit living and acting like the world, and follow the Lord: *If you abide in My word, you are My disciples indeed.*[4]

Journal - Personal notes, prayer points, & Scriptures you apply to this lesson.

Question: How would a person apply Hebrews 4:12 and 2 Tim. 3:16-17 for the purpose of self-control in order to avoid being controlled by the 'bayonet? What about Rom. 12:2?

_____

_____

60 Days Praying for America

DAY 18

Root Cuttings

> "In the case of *Rex v. Woolston*...the court said... whatever strikes at the root of Christianity, tends manifestly to the dissolution of civil government. The same doctrine was laid down in the late case of *The King v. Williams*... The authorities show that blasphemy against God, and contumelious reproaches and profane ridicule of Christ or the Holy Scriptures... are offenses punishable at common law... because it tends to corrupt the morals of the people and to destroy good order... They are treated as affecting the essential interests of civil society. We stand equally in need, now as formerly, of all the moral discipline, and of those principles of virtue, which help to bind society together." [1]

"WHATEVER STRIKES AT THE ROOT of Christianity, tends manifestly to the dissolution of civil government."

The judicial system has been whacking away at the root of Christianity's influence in American for many decades now, slowly but surely dissolving our civil government. The court decision issued above was written in 1811 by James Kent, Chief justice of the Supreme Court of the state of New York.

Court justices seem to have had a greater degree of wisdom in those days than they do today. In the days of James Kent, the law was immutable and unchanging. They viewed any government that wasn't supported by the moral principles of Christianity as being unstable. They did all they could to encouraged the principles of Christianity in the nation's populace in order to preserve civil government. In today's judicial system, there is no objective truth or stability in the law. The law is deemed flexible, something that can be contorted around prevailing societal and economic influences.

The licentiousness of moral relativism rules in today's judicial system. They continually whack away at the roots of Christianity, with the plain purpose of fragmenting government and society. As society begins to fragment and become more disruptive, chaos ensues. Out of chaos arises the opportunity for a tyrant to seize control; freedom and liberty are lost. Wittingly or unwittingly, this is the direction our current leaders and judges are taking American government and society.

> *A man* (or a nation) *is not established by wickedness, but the root of the righteous cannot be moved.*[2]

Christians are called upon to pray for these three groups: all men, kings, and all who are in authority.[3]

What America needs are judges and counselors just as we had at the beginning. Where are the Christians in the judicial system who will take a stand for the unchanging immutable principles of Christianity as outlined in the Bible?

What the church needs are leaders who will "*accommodate their discourses to the times, to preach against such sins as are most prevalent, and recommend such virtues as are most wanted.*"[4] Where are the leaders in pulpits who will take a stand for the unchanging principles of Christianity as outlined in the Bible?

What society needs are true Christians who will get in the Bible, learn God's righteous standards, stand up and speak out for those standards.

60 Days Praying for America

Journal - Personal notes, prayer points, & Scriptures you apply to this lesson.

Question: How do Proverbs 10:25 and Matthew 7:24-27 apply to America, the church, and society in this lesson?

DAY 19

Those Who Burn Incense

> "Moral habits...cannot safely be trusted on any other foundation than religious principle, nor any government be secure which is not supported by moral habits. Whatever makes men good Christians, makes them good citizens."[1]

FOR AMERICA TO HAVE THE TYPE OF GOVERNMENT needed to preserve the freedoms and liberties (not licentiousness) of its citizens, the citizens themselves must be virtuous. The best means of preserving virtue in the American people is by encouraging the biblical principles of Christian morality in the citizenry. All of the Founding Fathers frequently advocated this underlying principle:

"The good order and preservation of civil government, essentially depend upon piety, religion, and morality"[2] of a nation's citizens!

Furthermore, this principle for preserving a quality government and the liberties and freedoms it produces has been confirmed through our nation's history by many other of our leaders:

"Without a firm moral foundation, freedom degenerates quickly into selfishness and ... anarchy. Then there will be freedom only for the rapacious and those who are stronger and more unscrupulous than the rank and file of the people."[3]

60 Days Praying for America

In today's culture, claims of morality and accusations of immorality are tossed back and forth constantly between political parties. The Founding Fathers perceived this might be a problem. To prevent it, they encouraged the teaching of biblical moral principles in the educational system and the support and encouragement of good church leaders by state and federal governments. In that way, the people of America would know the difference between what is moral and immoral.

God says what He means and means what He says: *Righteousness exalts a nation, but sin is a reproach to any people.*[4]

In the old Roman Empire, worship of the emperor was compulsory. Each year, a Roman citizen was required to burn a pinch of incense on the altar and to acknowledge publicly that Caesar was supreme Lord. The action was intended simply as *proof of political loyalty* since the individual was permitted to worship whatever god or goddess he chose once he had offered to Caesar. This sounds very similar to many 'Christians' today. Prove your loyalty to your political party no matter what unrighteousness they promote: child sacrifice (abortion – the killing of babies, born or unborn), homosexuality, gender dysphoria, illegal immigration… whatever.

In America today, much as in the days of the early church, miscellaneous forces inside and outside of government work to prohibit God and His righteous standards in all aspects of our culture: education, media, judiciary, government, and society-at-large. Astonishingly, and shamefully, there are 'Christians' who adhere more loyally to the political party of their choice than they do to God and His standards of righteousness. They profess Jesus as their Lord, burn their pinch of inincense, yet bow their knee to their political party.

Many who are called leaders, political and otherwise, are destroying the foundation of biblical principles our government was founded upon. It is the church's responsibility to maintain that foundation, but many church leaders will not. As a result, America languishes under the reproach of sin.

Christians are supposed to be salt in the earth, not incense burners. What is required is for true Christians to get in the Bible, learn God's righteous standards, stand up and speak out for those standards, and quit bowing the knee to political parties when they are not aligned to biblical standards of righteousness.

Journal - Personal notes, prayer points, & Scriptures you apply to this lesson.

Question: Hosea 4:6 and Isaiah 5:13 indicate the consequences resulting from the lack of biblical morals. What Scriptures would help train people in the restoration of biblical morals?

_____

_____

_____

_____

_____

_____

_____

_____

_____

DAY 20

Crickets

> "It is the duty of the clergy to accommodate their discourses to the times, to preach against such sins as are most prevalent, and recommend such virtues as are most wanted... If exorbitant ambition and venality are predominant, ought they not to warn their hearers against those vices? If public spirit is much wanted, should they not inculcate this great virtue? If the rights and duties of Christian magistrates and subjects are disputed, should they not explain them, show their nature, ends, limitations, and restrictions, how much soever it may move the gall of [others]?"[1]

IT IS THE DUTY OF THE CLERGY to "accommodate their discourses to preach against such sins as are most prevalent…" Too many clergy today are making the wrong accommodations. Rather than preach against the sins that are prevalent in today's society, they make accommodations for the people who practice those sins.

In March of 2019, the leaders of the state of New York rejoiced in the passing of a law allowing the killing of babies right up to the moment of birth. There was no overwhelming outcry concerning this sin from the pulpits across America. It was shortly after this that the governor of Virginia promoted the passing of a law allowing the killing of babies *after they are born*! Both of these laws promote nothing less than human sacrifice.

The Preacher in Ecclesiastes stated that there is nothing new under the sun. Today's practice of killing babies, born or unborn, is the same abomination performed in the Old Testament of sacrificing living children to a false god by the name of Molech.[2] My, what a progressive, advanced, civilized society we have become.

How many 'Christians' heard their church leaders "accommodate their sermons to preach against this sin which is most prevalent" in the world today? (cricket… cricket…) If this coming Sunday, or sometime in the immediate future, your church leader fails to address the sin of child sacrifice, if all your church leader delivers are sermons on how to be happy in life, how to petition God for a new car, a new house, and a new spouse, that 'leader' is making accommodations for the sin of child sacrifice.

I know that seems like a hard statement, but it is true! God knows we all have need of cars, houses, and spouses. He said so: *Your heavenly Father knows that you need all these things.*[3] But those 'things' are *not* to be our focus. A Christian's focus should be to *seek first the kingdom of God and His righteousness.*[4] Abortion rights -child sacrifice – has nothing to do with righteousness. If Christians were to actually seek the Kingdom of God and His righteousness, <u>then</u> *all these things shall be added to you.* Want the 'things'? The reason we don't get the things is because we make too many accommodations for the sins.

It's been mentioned before: '*Good order and preservation of civil government, essentially depend upon piety, religion, and morality*' of America's citizens.

America needs your prayers. The *church* needs your prayers. If your church leaders are not "*accommodating their discourses to the times, to preach against such sins as are most prevalent,*" quit sitting around waiting for them. Get in your Bible and learn the truth. Stand up for that truth. Then get on your knees and pray. The power you have in the Spirit is far greater than any political power.

60 Days Praying for America

Journal - Personal notes, prayer points, & Scriptures you apply to this lesson.

Question: How would Isaiah 59:2-7 apply to the shedding of innocent blood as in abortions? Matthew 6:33 tells us to seek God's righteousness first. Where do we find God's righteousness?

60 Days Praying for America

DAY 21

You Get What You Pay For

> "Good order and preservation of civil government, essentially depend upon piety, religion, and morality... The legislature shall... require... suitable provision... for the institution of the public worship of God, and for the support and maintenance of public Protestant teachers of piety, religion, and morality."[1]

PAY ATTENTION! When you pay for something it generally means you're giving up one thing to obtain something else. Pay attention! That is a warning to quit focusing on the wrong thing and start focusing on the right thing. Pay attention! If you are willing to give up that, you will gain something of far more value. The question is, are you getting good value in what you're paying for?

A biblical example of paying attention would be in the comparison of Samuel to Eli and his sons. Samuel attended to – paid attention to – the things of the Lord. What did he get for the price he paid? God spoke to him and established him as a prophet of the Lord. Eli and his sons attended to – paid attention to – their own self-gratification. What did they get for the price they paid? The house of Eli and all of his sons fell into ruin, and none of Eli's descendants ever again held a priestly role in Israel.[2]

When America first started out as a nation, state legislatures were required to provide a 'suitable provision' – to pay for – "the institution of the public worship of God, and for the support and maintenance of public Protestant teachers of piety, religion and morality."

60 Days Praying for America

Pay attention! State legislatures were required to pay attention to the means of providing for "institutions for the public worship of God" and to pay for "public Protestant teachers of piety, religion, and morality." What did they expect to get for the price they paid? They expected to receive the "piety, religion, and morality of their citizens." Why was this worth the price they paid? Because the good order and preservation of civil government, essentially depend upon the piety, religion, and morality" of a nation's citizens! There was good value in what they paid for.

Pay attention! The "good order and preservation of civil government", which we see so lacking today, essentially depends on the "piety, religion, and morality" of that government's citizens.

Pay attention! America no longer attends to – pays attention to - this foundational principle of our nation. Instead, they pursue 'separation of church and state' and all the canard that goes with it.

Instead, like Eli and his sons, America's government and citizens are focused on their own self-gratification. What can America expect for the price it is paying? Ruin, just like Eli and his sons.

Pay attention! Can America avoid this? Yes. By attending to – paying attention to – the things of the Lord, just as Samuel did. If Americans "require... suitable provision... for the institution of the public worship of God, and for the support and maintenance of public Protestant teachers of piety, religion and morality," they will get what they pay for: "Good order and preservation of civil government."

60 Days Praying for America

Journal - Personal notes, prayer points, & Scriptures you apply to this lesson.

Question: Psalm 1 talks about 'paying attention.' How would you apply it to your life? How would you apply it to the church and the United States?

_____

_____

_____

_____

_____

_____

_____

_____

_____

_____

_____

_____

_____

_____

_____

_____

DAY 22

What Would Happen If...

> "I, Grover Cleveland, President of the United States, do hereby designate and set apart... a day of thanksgiving and prayer, to be observed by all the people of the land. On that day let all secular work and employment be suspended, and let our people assemble in their accustomed places of worship and with prayer and songs of praise give thanks to our Heavenly Father for all that He has done for us, while we humbly implore the forgiveness of our sins and a continuance of His mercy."[1]

DURING AMERICA'S HISTORY, our leaders made frequent calls for citizens to:

1. Humble themselves before God.
2. Pray.
3. Seek God.
4. Quit sinning.

President Grover Cleveland's call is one such example. But this doesn't happen so much anymore.

> It is unconstitutional for a high school to open their football game with prayer.[2]

Whereas formerly, the call was to pray, the call now is to quit praying.

60 Days Praying for America

For many decades American citizens have been dissuaded from even mentioning God, let alone from seeking him or of "giving thanks for all that He has done for us while we humbly implore the forgiveness of our sins."

For many decades now, politicians have promised to deal with the issue of freedom of religion in all aspects of society, but have twiddled away the time, never seriously applying themselves to fulfilling that promise.

For many decades now, judges in America's judicial system have issued decisions pushing God farther and farther out of government, education, entertainment and media, and out of society-at-large.

For many decades now, Christians have sat calmly in their pews, satisfied to worship God inside the four walls of their church just as long as the status quo was maintained - or at least appeared to be maintained - outside their church.

Citizens, politicians, judges, churches. Which one of these groups is personally responsible and will be held accountable for upholding God's proper place in American culture?

The church. As the church goes, so goes America. The truth of the matter is that citizens, politicians, and judges have muddled their way along for many decades, and will continue to muddle their way along for many decades into the future, attempting to perpetuate the status quo.

But the time is now for those in the church who are truly called by His name, not those who claim to be Christian yet show no evidence of living as a Christian, to answer the call given in the opening quote.

God said, *If My people who are called by My name...* That narrows it down even further than the level of the church. God is talking to *you!* "If *you*, Christian, who claim to be called by My name, will 1) humble yourself before Me, 2) pray, 3) seek Me, and 4) quit sinning, then I will hear from heaven, forgive *your* sins, and heal your land."[3]

60 Days Praying for America

What would happen if:

… students in the schools of America stood up and said, "We don't care what the judges say; we are opening our football games with prayer?"

… students, of their own accord, brought their own Bibles into their classroom?

… students, of their own accord, prayed earnestly in school?

… students, of their own accord, posted the Ten Commandments on their book covers, lockers, t-shirts?

… students, of their own accord, committed to serving Jesus Christ and living by His Word?

If students truly want something to rebel about, if they truly want a cause to start a revolution over, let them demand the return of God, His Word, prayer, and the Ten Commandments in their classrooms.

It would be a second American Revolution that would restore the foundation of the liberties of this nation, the liberties that only the God of the Bible provides for all mankind.

It is time for real Christians to answer their Lord's call to *deny yourself, take up your cross and follow Me*.[4]

Journal - Personal notes, prayer points, & Scriptures you apply to this lesson.

Question: List six positive Scripture verses that talk about seeking God. How will you personally apply these verses in your life?

_____

_____

_____

_____

60 Days Praying for America

DAY 23

Diluted & Deluded

> "Independent of its connection with human destiny hereafter, the fate of republican [form of] government is indissolubly bound up with the fate of the Christian religion, and a people who reject its holy faith will find themselves the slaves of their own evil passions and of arbitrary power."[1]

> Reciting "under God" in the Pledge of Allegiance in public schools is an unconstitutional endorsement of religion.[2]

MANY WOULD OBSERVE that the "fate of the Christian religion" has been on the wane for several decades now. It's interesting the author of the opening quote, a former presidential candidate, would make the astute observation that the "fate of America's government is *indissolubly* bound with the fate of Christian religion." If the Christian religion has been waning for decades, then America's government is in a most difficult situation.

In some churches, people who perhaps might be sincere Christians are allowed to bring all of their old myths, philosophies, and prejudices with them right into the church. Rather than take on the discipline required to align themselves with God's will as revealed in His Word, they are allowed to continue in their old ways and habits. This brings far too much mixture into the church. Rather than offend new Christians, Scripture is diluted, allowing them to hold on with sympathy to their old passions instead of *denying themselves, taking up their cross and following Jesus*.[3] Dilution always brings delusion.

60 Days Praying for America

If this is the current "fate of the Christian religion", why should we be surprised that our government allows illegal aliens into the country without any training or requirement for learning their rights and responsibilities to become contributing citizens? The same destruction that Christians have allowed to take place in the church is now taking place in America's government. "The fate of America's government is indissolubly bound up with the fate of the Christian religion!" It seems both the Church and America are diluted and deluded. That delusion has led us to be *"slaves of our own evil passions and of arbitrary power."*

The Apostle Paul knew what he was doing when he prayed for the church: *For this reason we... do not cease to pray for you... that you may walk worthy of the Lord... fully pleasing Him... increasing in the knowledge of God.*[4] This prayer should be prayed more frequently by more true Christians. Do you call yourself a Christian? Great. First, *deny yourself, take up your cross and follow Jesus.* Then pray *that we might turn from our iniquities and understand God's truth.*[5]

Journal - Personal notes, prayer points, & Scriptures you apply to this lesson.

Question: How would 2 Corinthians 6:14-18; Galatians 2:20; and Colossians 3:23 apply to this lesson and to your life?

_____

_____

_____

_____

_____

60 Days Praying for America

DAY 24

Sum Of All Fears

> "He therefore is the truest friend to the liberty of his country who tries most to promote its virtue, and who, so far as his power and influence extend, will not suffer a man to be chosen into any office of power and trust who is not a wise and virtuous man.
>
> We must not conclude merely upon a man's haranguing upon liberty, and using the charming sound, that he is fit to be trusted with the liberties of his country. It is not unfrequent to hear men declaim loudly upon liberty who, if we may judge by the whole tenor of their actions, mean nothing else by it but their own liberty, — to oppress without control or the restraint of laws all who are poorer or weaker than themselves.
>
> It is not, I say, unfrequent to see such instances, though at the same time I esteem it a justice due to my country to say that it is not without shining examples of the contrary kind; — examples of men of a distinguished attachment to this same liberty I have been describing; whom no hopes could draw, no terrors could drive, from steadily pursuing, in their sphere, the true interests of their country; whose fidelity has been tried in the nicest and tenderest manner, and has been ever firm and unshaken.
>
> The sum of all is, if we would most truly enjoy this gift of Heaven, let us become a virtuous people."[1]

60 Days Praying for America

POLITICAL CANDIDATES, along with most other people, are capable of waxing eloquent concerning liberty. But as the speaker above noted, there are two types of people who discuss liberty.

There are those who, when they elaborate upon liberty, merely mean their own liberty. The liberty that allows them to control and suppress others while they themselves remain above the law. They do this by offering the public a kind of pseudo-liberty, promising government and corporate handouts. Their discourse on this self-promoting liberty sounds so well-meaning and compassionate. But they are doing nothing more than depriving persons of their individual liberty and replacing it with subservience as a slave to a master. To safeguard their own liberty, they create new laws which they themselves have no inclination or intention of submitting to. Following the principles of Machiavellianism, they never keep their word "when by doing so it would be against their interests."[2]

Then there are those who understand that true liberty comes only from the God of the Bible. These are the ones who realize that the more people look to other men to provide for them, to rule over and protect them, the more they slump from liberty to bondage.

They know that true liberty can only come from God. They understand that no man can serve two masters; he cannot serve both man and God. He will end up loving the One and hating the other, or hating the One and loving the other. Only by loving God can a man obtain true liberty and thus truly love his fellow man.

To obtain true liberty man must serve God. Whenever you attempt to serve man and submit to man's rule for the purpose of provision and protection, all liberty is lost. Then you have no recourse but to crouch down and lick the hand that feeds you.

The fear of the first is that of being found out and held responsible for his suppression of others and for his own disregard of the law. The fear of the second is the fear – the reverence - of God, which is the beginning of wisdom and the foundation of true liberty.

As stated above, the sum of it all is this: if we would truly enjoy liberty, which is a gift from God not from man, then we must submit ourselves to God and not to man. We must become a virtuous people according to biblical principles of Christianity.

"He therefore is the truest friend to the liberty of his country who tries most to promote its virtue…"

Journal - Personal notes, prayer points, & Scriptures you apply to this lesson.

Question: 2 Timothy 3:1-5 talks about the conditions of society in the last days. How do these verses apply to this lesson? How can we comprehending and apply the truths found in the Bible and avoid being deceived by political jargon?

_____

_____

_____

_____

_____

_____

_____

_____

60 Days Praying for America

DAY 25

Sowing Seed

> "Let the youth of America ... instead of indulging a rapturous admiration for the modern superficial speechifyers in favor of an American monarchy, [i.e. social media users who rant in favor of centralized all-powerful socialist government] let them examine the principles of the late glorious revolution ... [i.e. the American Revolution of 1776] and before they embrace the chains of servitude, let them scrutinize ... if their pride ... will suffer them to lick the hand of a despotic master ... Let the old Patriots come forward... let them lift up the voice like a trumpet, and show this people their folly and ... impending danger."[1]

WHY DO SO MANY of America's youth favor socialism today? 48% against capitalism and 51% favoring socialism, according to a recent poll. It has to do with seeds. Jesus plainly taught that God's Word is Seed.[2] Words are seeds in that they instigate a process of thinking in a person. Some seeds are good, other seeds are bad.

"Public schools exist to educate, not to proselytize. Children in public schools are a captive audience. Making prayer an official part of the school day is coercive and invasive."[3]

This is an official statement of an organization called Freedom from Religion. These are people who do not understand that in truth they've always had freedom from religion. Even America's Founding Fathers recognized that a decision to follow the teachings of Jesus Christ as taught in the Bible is a personal decision and that the State has no authority to coerce a person to make that decision.

At the same time, the Founding Fathers recognized that the only means of securing the God-given liberties outlined in the Declaration of Independence and the Constitution lays in the personal morality of each individual citizen of our country. So, they made every effort to promote the teachings of biblical morality in schools and churches, as well as promoting them in the halls of government. Once people had been presented with the teaching of biblical principles, it was up to each individual to make a personal decision to live by those teachings. There was never any coercion on the part of the government. Students were given information so they could make their own choice.

Over many decades groups like this have been successful in removing Bible teaching, prayer, the Ten Commandments and so forth, not just from school rooms, but from government and society. They have succeeded in removing the Seed of the Word of God from the hearts and minds of America's youth. They have robbed American youth of their freedom. The freedom to decide for themselves whether they should live by biblical standards of morality, the same freedom sought so diligently by America's Founding Fathers.

In its place, they plant diversity seeds and tolerance seeds, the seeds of moral relativism; there is no universal truth that can be applied to everyone. Truth is what you decide it is. God's morality is irrelevant. Teaching students this, without comparing it to biblical teaching, is coercive.

All Christians are called to be Seed sowers. If we are not allowed to plant Seed in the schoolroom, then plant it in the home, plant Seed on the campus everywhere outside the schoolroom, plant Seed at work, plant Seed wherever your sphere of influence is.

Planting Seed is simple. You don't have to preach a sermon. Plant seeds one-at-a-time. Simply make comments on biblical truth in your conversations. Those who are curious and seekers will ask you questions. From there you can water the Seed and watch it grow.

We must be like the disciples. They went out and preached - they sowed Seed – everywhere![4] We must sow Seed everywhere!

Journal - Personal notes, prayer points, & Scriptures you apply to this lesson.

Question: When it comes to the decision God gives us to make in Deuteronomy 30:19, why do so many make the wrong decision? Proverbs 4:23 says we should guard our heart, for out of it spring the issues of life. What other verses show us the kind of commitment required to love, honor, and serve only the Lord?

_____

_____

_____

_____

_____

_____

_____

_____

_____

60 Days Praying for America

DAY 26

Oil & Water

> "The church in the West has suffered a defeat of great magnitude, and its civilization based on Judeo-Christian foundations has collapsed. In its place, the West, without exception, now lives and functions as a pagan world. A pagan worldview and a pagan lifestyle now prevail. Thus, the church in the West, and everywhere else in the world, exists in the midst of pagan controlled surroundings and is called upon to live and witness to a hostile world that is opposed to all Christianity stands for, and against which it wages unceasing war. How then should the church and its people live? What should the church's role be? And what about its long-range objectives?"[1]

BY AND LARGE, THIS IS THE CHALLENGE facing America today. The Founding Fathers had a firm understanding that the only thing securing the American form of government - a Constitutional Republic - and the liberties our government secures, is the morality of individual citizens. They also understood that the only thing securing an individual's morality is the teaching of biblical Christianity.

You hear it stated often that Jesus said, "The gates of Hades shall not prevail against the church." Actually, He never said that and He never taught that. The lesson He taught His disciples went like this:

He said to them, "But who do you say that I am?" Simon Peter answered and said, "You are the Christ, the Son of the living God." Jesus answered and said to him, "Blessed are you, Simon Bar-Jonah, for flesh and blood has not revealed this to you, but My Father who is in heaven. And I also say to you that you are Peter, and on this rock – not on Peter, but on the revelation that Jesus is the Christ - *I will build My church, and the gates of Hades shall not prevail against* – the church that builds on the revelation that Jesus is the Christ."[2]

To reiterate, here is what Jesus said:

- The Rock is the revelation that Jesus is the Christ.
- On this Rock – the revelation that Jesus is the Christ -Jesus will build His Church.
- The gates of Hades will not prevail against the Rock – the revelation that Jesus is the Christ.
- Nor will the gates of Hades prevail against the church built upon the Rock – the revelation that Jesus is the Christ.

Jesus is both the foundation and the head of His church.[3] At no point did Jesus cede these roles to Peter or any of His other disciples.

Many 'Christian' churches have quit building on the Rock, and America suffers for it.

In addition to declaring that He would build His church on the rock, Jesus also taught that those who are wise will build on the Rock, and those who are fools will build on the sand. He said if you build on the Rock, your house – church and nation – will stand in the face of any adversity. He said if you build on the sand, your house – church and nation – will be destroyed in the face of any adversity. Then He said that you build your house – church and nation – on the Rock by "hearing and obeying His Word."[4]

Today many churches try to build on the sand of diversity and the 'tolerance gospel.' These churches try to please and accept everybody, no matter their behavior or lifestyle. They claim this is biblical love in action. God loves everybody, they say. That's true.[5] Therefore, they say, God loves and accepts the homosexual, transgendered, and those of other lifestyles that are at odds with biblical righteousness, and we should welcome them and their lifestyles into our church. Sorry. No.

God never compromises His standards of righteousness, nor does He wink at sin. Yes, it is true God sent His Son to pay the penalty for your sins (and mine!). But once a person is genuinely born-again God expects them to change their words, actions, and lifestyle to conform to His standards.[6]

Allowing people with sinful behaviors and lifestyles into the culture of the church is not showing love to those people. It is tolerating their sin, which is the very thing we are commanded not to do. Yes, God loves mankind. But He will never tolerate mankind's sinful behavior and lifestyle.

In the complete teaching of the proper way to *love your neighbor as yourself*, God said, *You shall not hate your brother in your heart. You shall surely rebuke your neighbor, and not bear* – tolerate - *sin because of him.*[7]

Listen: tolerating your neighbor's immoral lifestyle is wrong! Christians are supposed to stand for biblical morality, not tolerate aberrations of biblical morality. If a neighbor - anyone you might happen to know - is involved in an immoral behavior or lifestyle, as a Christian you are not supposed to ignore it. You are supposed to warn them of both the immediate and eternal consequences of their behavior.

You shall not take vengeance, nor bear any grudge against the children of your people, but you shall love your neighbor as yourself: I am the LORD.[8]

Should your neighbor choose to ignore your warnings, you are not to condemn them or take vengeance, nor bear any grudge against them. You are to continue showing them the love of God and to continue declaring the truth of His Word to them.

60 Days Praying for America

Christians are required to rise far above the tolerance gospel. They are required to love their neighbors, love their enemies, and forgive those who do them harm. But Christians are never to tolerate sin. Martin Luther King put it this way, "Darkness cannot drive out darkness: only light can do that. Hate cannot drive out hate: only love can do that."[9]

God put it this way, *Love does not rejoice in iniquity, but rejoices in the truth. Love never fails!*[10]

Tolerance always fails. In order to build on the Rock churches and Christians must hear and obey this lesson in God's Word. Like oil and water, tolerance and God's standard of righteousness do not mix.

Journal - Personal notes, prayer points, & Scriptures you apply to this lesson.

Question: Psalm 119:113; James 1:5-8; 4:8-10 talk about double-mindedness, or tolerance. How would you apply these verses to this lesson? How would you apply these verses in praying for America?

_____

_____

_____

_____

_____

_____

_____

_____

60 Days Praying for America

60 Days Praying for America

DAY 27

Lights & Baskets

> "Tyranny, like hell, is not easily conquered; yet we have this consolation with us that the harder the conflict, the more glorious the triumph" [1]

TYRANNY, LIKE HELL, fights against God-given liberties. But, the gates of Hades shall not prevail against the church. Right?

The Founding Fathers had a firm understanding that the only thing securing the American form of government - a Constitutional-Republic - and the liberties secured by that government, is the moral character of each individual citizen. The Founders also understood that the only thing securing the morality of an individual is the promotion and teaching of biblical Christianity.

The plan of Hell and tyranny is to weaken and de-legitimize the church's influence in people's lives. They accomplish this by removing Bibles and Bible teaching in schools. Nor is prayer allowed in school. No Bible or prayer is allowed in government settings (where they are needed the most!) No Bible or prayer is allowed in public discourse. The only place hell and tyrants even consider allowing the Bible and prayer is inside the four walls of a church. You know, hidden under a bushel basket. Yet Jesus told Christians to do just the opposite: *You are the light of the world. A city that is set on a hill cannot be hidden. Nor do they light a lamp and put it under a basket, but on a lampstand, and it gives light to all who are in the house. Let your light so shine before men, that they may see your good works and glorify your Father in heaven.*[2]

60 Days Praying for America

In light of the strategy of hell and tyranny, it is critically important for individual Christians to study the Bible for themselves. To find out what the Bible says on the issues of our day – abortion, sexual immorality, and so forth - and to do three things with those principles:

- Live by them.
- Stand up publicly for them.
- Pray for America and our neighbors.

As Christians, we are not to rationalize or equivocate on biblical standards of a godly lifestyle, we are to live by them and promote them. We are to demand the same of our elected officials, and we are to vote according to biblical principles, not according to the political party we happen to favor. We are to favor God's principles of biblical morality over and above all political party affiliations.

Hell and tyrants know that if they can keep the Bible and prayer inside a church – hidden under a bushel basket, then they have just removed the influence of the Word of God from all other arenas. The only problem for hell and tyrants is this: Jesus never said, "The gates of Hades shall not prevail against the church." What He said was, "The gates of hell shall not prevail against the Rock, nor against the church built upon the Rock." The Rock is the revelation that Jesus is the Christ. It is time for Christians to begin building their lives on that Rock by both hearing and following God's Word.

> "The summer soldier and the sunshine patriot will, in this crisis, shrink from the service of their country; but he that stands by it now, deserves the love and thanks of man and woman. Tis the business of little minds to shrink; but he whose heart is firm, and whose conscience approves his conduct, will pursue his principles unto death…"[3]

The summer disciples and the sunshine Christians will, in this crisis, shrink from the service of their Lord, Jesus Christ. They will allow society and pop-culture to influence them more than they influence society and pop-culture. They will shrink from pursuing the principles of biblical morality – from building on the Rock. But *Those who know their God will be strong and carry out great exploits!*[4]

Journal - Personal notes, prayer points, & Scriptures you apply to this lesson.

Question: In Matthew 5:13-16 we are told that as Christians we should be salt and light in the world. How do Proverbs 4:18-19; John 8:12; 1 Peter 2:11-12 and Philippians 2:14-16 also apply in this lesson?

_____

_____

_____

_____

_____

_____

_____

_____

_____

_____

DAY 28

Kindergarteners vs. Judges - Heads Up!

> "Let every student be plainly instructed and earnestly pressed to consider well the main end of his life and studies is to know God and Jesus Christ which is eternal life, John 17:3, and therefore to lay Christ in the bottom, as the only foundation of all sound knowledge and learning... seeing the Lord only giveth wisdom, let everyone seriously set himself by prayer in secret to seek it of Him. Proverbs 2, 3... Everyone shall exercise himself in reading the Scriptures twice a day, that he shall be ready to give such account of his proficiency therein."[1]

> "It is unconstitutional for a kindergarten class to ask during a school assembly whose birthday is celebrated by Christmas."[2]

I'M SURE ALL KINDERGARTENERS are aware of their accountability to avoid violating a supposed constitutional precept. Except this is a judicial farce since the Constitution has no jurisdiction over schools, let alone kindergarten classes. The judges involved in this 'judicial' decision were apparently completely ignorant of their own accountability before the Supreme Judge to see to it that children are taught about God: *Whoever causes one of these little ones who believe in Me to sin, it would be better for him if a millstone were hung around his neck, and he were drowned in the depth of the sea.*[3] Just a heads up, judges.

Education was performed properly at one time, as evidenced at the beginning of Harvard University in the opening quote. Things have changed for the worse since then. However, the real responsibility for a godly education falls on the parents. So… when will it be time for Christian parents to ignore the misconceptions of judges and the judicial system, and stand up for the Truth?

Therefore you shall lay up these words of mine in your heart and in your soul… You shall teach them to your children, speaking of them when you sit in your house, when you walk by the way, when you lie down, and when you rise up.[4]

Or will we continue in this vein:

They have regarded and broken Your law as void… They devise evil by law… They serve their own gods according to their judicial verdicts…[5]

Professing to be wise, they became fools…[6]

Journal - Personal notes, prayer points, & Scriptures you apply to this lesson.

Question: What is your answer to the question: When will it be time for Christian parents to ignore the misconceptions of judges and the judicial system, and stand up for the Truth? Provide a Scriptural basis for your answer.

_____

_____

_____

_____

_____

_____

_____

60 Days Praying for America

DAY 29

Dreams & Kingdoms

Benjamin Rush said,

"The only foundation for a useful education in a republic is to be laid in religion [Christianity]. Without this there can be no virtue, and without virtue there can be no liberty, and liberty is the object and life of all republican governments."[1]

James Otis asked and answered,

"Has [government] any foundation? Any chief cornerstone? ... it has an everlasting foundation in the unchangeable will of God... The sum of my argument is that civil government is of God."[2]

John Adams declared it quite clearly,

"It is religion [Christianity] and morality alone which can establish the principles upon which freedom can securely stand. The only foundation of a free constitution is pure virtue."[3]

And George Washington concluded,

"Of all the dispositions and habits which lead to political prosperity, religion [Christianity] and morality are indispensable supports."[4]

DIFFERENT TYPES OF GOVERNMENTS have different types of foundations. America's form of government, a Constitutional Republic, has a specific foundation. Do you know what that foundation is? Yes? No?

60 Days Praying for America

Maybe, but you're not sure? Well, several of our Founding Fathers told us succinctly what the foundation of our constitutional republic is.

People and politicians talk a lot about pursuing the "American Dream." But, is the pursuit of the "American Dream" ruining our nation? Just what is the "American Dream?

According to Investopedia, "The American Dream is the belief that anyone, regardless of where they were born or what class they were born into, can attain their own version of success in a society where upward mobility is possible for everyone. The American Dream is achieved through sacrifice, risk-taking, and hard work, rather than by chance."[5]

"The dream that everyone can achieve their own version of success." Okay, what is "success"? Everyone has their own definition of success. For some, success is starting a business and building it into a self-sustaining personal economic system. For others, success is getting a job that lets them pay the bills. For still others, success is laying around and living off the largess of those who actually do work. For most people, success is the attainment of whatever it is, good or bad, that makes them happy.

For most people today, "the pursuit of happiness" is wrapped around self-achievement, self-gratification, and self-fulfillment. Self comes first in every situation. In our "pursuit of happiness, there is a bottom-line question that must be considered. Our Founding Fathers made it perfectly clear that the foundation of our government, our liberty, and therefore our way of life is found *only* in living by the principles of Christian morality. That is the only means of producing virtue in the public. Public virtue is the only means of preserving the liberties our form of government provides.

The question then is this: in our endless pursuit of the American Dream have we neglected the foundation of our nation - living by biblical principles of morality? It would appear so.

60 Days Praying for America

Is it wrong to attempt to achieve success through business? Only if we pursue that kind of success to the neglect of all else. God said He would help us be successful if we seek Him first: *But seek first the kingdom of God and His righteousness, and all these things shall be added to you.*[6] We can only give our heart, soul, mind, and strength to the pursuit of one desire, either to God or to the American Dream. In giving our heart, soul, mind, and strength to the American Dream we become blinded by our own selfish greed and lusts. Once we cease to live by biblical principles of morality, we lose our virtue. Once we lose our virtue the foundation of our nation crumbles.

Living by the principles of biblical morality leads to virtue. Virtue leads to liberty. Liberty is the object and life of all republican governments. Our dreams or His Kingdom? The people who founded our nation's government did their best to encourage us to make the right choice.

Journal - Personal notes, prayer points, & Scriptures you apply to this lesson.

Question: What do Job 5:17; Psalm 128:2; Proverbs 3:13, 18; 16:20; 28:14 and 28:18 say about the "pursuit of happiness?" How do Matthew 6:24-25, 33; Philippians 4:19; and James 4:4 apply to this lesson? When do work and the desire for gain come into odds with your relationship with God?

_____

_____

_____

_____

_____

_____

60 Days Praying for America

DAY 30

To Acquire & Secure

> "When we view the blessings with which our country has been favored, those which we now enjoy, and the means which we possess of handing them down unimpaired to our latest posterity, our attention is irresistibly drawn to the source from whence they flow. Let us then, unite in offering our most grateful acknowledgments for these blessings to the Divine Author of All Good."[1]

WE USED TO BE ABLE TO "hand them down unimpaired to our latest prosperity" until laws began to be passed such as: "If a student prays over his lunch, it is unconstitutional for him to pray aloud."[2]

Our country has been favored with blessings. But feebleminded reasoning such as this judicial decision greatly impedes our ability to pass those blessings on to our offspring. And no matter the efforts we may make, individually or jointly in and of ourselves, we are incapable of either producing or securing those same blessings that were obtained by our forefathers as they repented of their sins and sought the God of the Bible. For that is the true source of these blessings. And our "grateful acknowledgment to Him for these blessings" is the only means of securing them.

Benjamin Rush, a signer of the Declaration of Independence, wrote his autobiography for his children, in which he hoped to "prevent my children from being deceived by the histories of this day." In his writings he relates an experience he had with John Adams:

60 Days Praying for America

"I sat next to John Adams in Congress, and upon my whispering to him and asking him if he thought we should succeed in our struggle with Great Britain, he answered me, *'Yes - if we fear God and repent of our sins.'*"[3]

In our struggle today, we can re-gain and re-secure "the blessings with which our country has been favored" if we will do the same and – unhampered - thank God for them at every opportunity.

They have regarded and broken Your law as void…
They devise evil by law…

They serve their own gods according to their judicial verdicts…[4]

Professing to be wise, they became fools…[5]

We make our prayer before the LORD our God,
that we might turn from our iniquities and understand Your truth.[6]

Journal - Personal notes, prayer points, & Scriptures you apply to this lesson.

Question: Read Deuteronomy 6:5-7. Courts, schools, churches. Who is responsible for children's education? Read Mark 9:42 and 19:24. Why is Jesus so serious about this issue?

_____

_____

_____

_____

_____

60 Days Praying for America

60 Days Praying for America

DAY 31

Lowering This Raises That

> "To a man of liberal education, the study of history is not only useful, and important, but altogether indispensable, and with regard to the history contained in the Bible it is not so much praiseworthy to be acquainted with as it is shameful to be ignorant of it."[1]

> "Freedom of speech and press is guaranteed to students unless the topic is religious, at which time such speech becomes unconstitutional."[2]

JOHN WITHERSPOON was a signer of the Declaration of Independence. By age four he had read the Bible from cover to cover. And as a young child, he could recite most of the New Testament. Another founder who had read the entire Bible by age four was John Trumbull, a justice on the Supreme Court of New Jersey. Harriet Beecher Stowe had memorized twenty-seven hymns and several chapters of the Bible by the time she had reached the age of seven.

A school teacher once held a contest in his classroom, offering a brand new pocket knife to the student who could memorize the most Bible verses over the weekend. The following Monday a young boy stood and recited some sixty or seventy verses before he was stopped and the knife was handed to him. That boy, Daniel Webster, said he had several other chapters he had also learned.

60 Days Praying for America

Fisher Ames, a member of the first federal Congress who helped frame the Bill of Rights, had also read the Bible as a youngster and began studying Latin at age six. After passing the entrance exam, he entered Harvard at age twelve, graduated when he was sixteen and became a teacher.

The Bible was the primary textbook in our schools for centuries. As a result, American schools produced the nation's finest military commanders, teachers, businessmen, ministers, scientists, and statesmen.

At age eight, the son of this founding Father was the official secretary to his father on his diplomatic trip to France. At age thirteen he traveled with his father to Holland where he attended Leiden University. At age fourteen became the French interpreter and secretary for America's ambassador to Russia. At age sixteen he became secretary to the American commissioners in France who were negotiating the treaty with Great Britain to end the Revolutionary War. He was John Quincy Adams, son of John Adams. Oh! He also became the sixth President of the United States.

Were John Quincy Adams and the others mentioned above just smarter than everyone else? No. During this period of American history, biblical principles of education were followed. Expectations for the students were raised with the understanding that the student would rise to meet those expectations. Today's educational system promotes entitlement over expectation, social policies over individual achievement.

Today's educational system is one of reduced standards where expectations are lowered. As long as a student does something, homework and test scores cannot be below 50, and no lower than 40 if they did nothing. Students are allowed to re-take a test nearly as often as they like. Late work from the beginning of the semester can be turned in at the end of the semester. And guess what? Students have lowered themselves to fulfill those expectations!

60 Days Praying for America

The fear of the Lord is the beginning of wisdom.[3] Real education begins with the Bible. And as the opening quote points out, *"To a man of liberal education... it is shameful to be ignorant of the Bible!"*

Journal - Personal notes, prayer points, & Scriptures you apply to this lesson.

Question: We often form expectations automatically. It's part of our thought process. Every good coach will require daily improvement on the part of his players. On the other hand, when it comes to raising children, many parents do not. Epheisans 4:24 and 2 Timothy 3:16-17 talk about standards. How do those verses fit here?

_____

_____

_____

_____

_____

_____

_____

_____

_____

_____

_____

DAY 32

Not The Same

> "If a republican [form of] government fails to secure public prosperity and happiness, it must be because the citizens neglect the divine commands, and elect bad men to make and administer the laws."[1]

Liberty: freedom of expression under the restrictions of a moral code (in America's case, the moral code of Christianity.)

Licentiousness: freedom unrestrained by law or morality; lawless; immoral.

PEOPLE AND POLITICIANS (not that politicians aren't people) talk about 'liberty' and 'freedom' in the same breath. While the terms are synonymous, they are not entirely the same thing.

Freedom is described as the license, the permission, to do whatever you please no matter if it is right or wrong, moral or immoral. In the 1960s the cry for freedom was, 'If it feels good, do it!' Actually, that adage has been around for as long as there have been people. Freedom in that sense gives no consideration as to whether 'it' is right or wrong, moral or immoral. As long as 'it' feels good to you, do 'it.' But there's a catch, especially as freedom applies to people in today's society.

Freedom is the permission to do something. Permission is necessarily granted by someone in authority. If the person in authority can grant permission, then they can also revoke permission. In American society today, too many people are demanding permission to do whatever they want without being restrained by any moral standard. To achieve this goal, they attempt to elect anyone to government leadership who will give them permission for the freedom to be licentious. They work to elect bad men to make and administer laws which allow them to "neglect the divine commandments." Fair warning: the State giveth and the State taketh away! Under that type of governance, your 'freedoms' are always at risk.

Liberty, on the other hand, is referred to in the Declaration of Independence: 'all men are endowed by their Creator with certain inalienable rights.' Liberty doesn't come from men; it comes from God. Because God-given liberty is 'inalienable' it cannot be taken away from the individual by any man or by any government. The only instance in which your liberties and rights can be revoked is by your own choice – when you attempt to interfere with the rights of others and the government has to step in to protect the other person's liberty.

Because liberty can only be revoked by the choice of the individual, it requires personal stewardship on the part of the individual. Each citizen of the United States must be self-governed by a moral code. Also, each individual will be responsible to give account to God for how they lived by that code in order to protect their God-given liberties. The moral code which the Founding Fathers recommended and made every effort to secure was biblical Christianity.

Freedom and liberty are not the same. In regards to the opening quote, too many people today are libertines. Refusing to be constrained by the divine commands, they elect bad men to make the laws which they falsely believe will give them freedom to do whatever makes them feel good. Libertines should be prepared to face the ramifications of their actions. If you refuse to be ruled by God, you will be ruled by men who act as tyrants, granting and revoking your 'freedoms' at their whim, never securing public prosperity and happiness. And in the end of it all, you will be required to stand before God and give an account of why you thought it wise to pursue licentious desires that are contrary to His moral code.

Journal - Personal notes, prayer points, & Scriptures you apply to this lesson.

Question: What does John 8:34 say is the condition of people who practice sin? Many Christians today believe they are free to do whatever they want and God will still forgive them because Jesus died to pay the penalty for their sins. How does Romans 6:15-19 correct your thinking about this issue? Christians are told be "overcomers" – Romans 12:21; 1 John 4:4; 5:4-5. Are you an Overcomer, or have you been overcome by sin? Can you find other verses on being an Overcomer? How does this lesson apply to America?

_____

_____

_____

_____

_____

_____

_____

_____

DAY 33

"What Difference Does It Make?"

> "Evangelicalism in America has been transformed from a counterculture to merely a subculture. Evangelical Christianity is being reduced to a mirror image of the larger culture. We embrace the same values, work for the same goals, and live for the same reasons as our non-believing neighbors, all the while professing that we are citizens of the Kingdom of God."[1]

IT'S DIFFICULT TO CONVINCE YOUR NEIGHBOR, co-worker, family, friends, or buddies at the gym that Jesus can make a difference in their lives when there is little to no difference between your lifestyle and theirs. Everyone lives in a hectic, anxiety-filled world today. How can other people wonder what gives Christians hope if Christians whine and gripe about the same anxieties instead of demonstrating how they overcame those anxieties? How can others wonder what gives a Christian hope if Christians share the same worldly values they do instead of demonstrating biblical values? The Bible says talk is cheap. It's time to be overcomers:

My language and my message were not set forth in persuasive, enticing, and plausible words of wisdom, but they were in demonstration of the Holy Spirit and power, a proof by the Spirit and power of God, operating on me and stirring in the minds of my hearers the emotions and thus persuading them. So that your faith might not rest in human philosophy, but in the power of God.[2]

60 Days Praying for America

It's past time for Christians to quit mimicking the world. If you have a blue flashlight and everyone else in the room has a blue flashlight, no one is going to sit up and take notice. But, if you've got a red flashlight, everyone will notice. Living by the biblical principles of Christianity is what made America great for nearly two centuries. Giving up biblical principles of Christianity and taking on the culture and values of the world is what is making America weak and insignificant.

You are the light of the world. A city set on a hill cannot be hidden. Nor do men light a lamp and put it under a bushel basket, but on a lampstand, and it gives light to all in the house. Let your light so shine before men that they may see your moral excellence and your praiseworthy, noble, and good deeds and recognize and honor and praise and glorify your Father Who is in heaven.[3]

Therefore, come out from among them and be separate, says the Lord.[4] That doesn't mean quit hanging around people, it means quit acting like them! Too many Christians these days are mixed up – with the world!

Journal - Personal notes, prayer points, & Scriptures you apply to this lesson.

Question: God does not compromise on His standards of righteousness. How do 2 John 1:9-11 and 1 Tim. 6:11-12 apply to this compromise - tolerance - when it comes to living the Christian lifestyle?

_____

_____

_____

_____

60 Days Praying for America

60 Days Praying for America

DAY 34

Pluralism Never Unites

> "Moral habits…cannot safely be trusted on any other foundation than religious principle, nor any government be secure which is not supported by moral habits. Whatever makes men good Christians, makes them good citizens."[1]

> "These, and many other matters which might be noticed, add a volume of unofficial declarations to the mass of organic utterances that this is a Christian nation."[2]

WELL… THE UNITED STATES used to be a Christian nation. But now the shifting foundational sands of religious pluralism have set in. It becomes more and more difficult to speak against any religion… except Christianity. The problem is all religions do not lead to the same end. Consider that Jehovah is not Allah, and Allah is not Jehovah. The two are diametrically opposed to each other. They have nothing in common:

1. Jesus died for the benefit of all men. Jesus Christ died on the Cross for ALL mankind. That would include Muslims, Arabs, Buddhists, Hindus, all races and creeds of mankind; no one is left out. Mohammed died, but not for the benefit of anyone in particular.

2. God sent His Son Jesus to die for all men. God so loved the world that He sent His only begotten Son to die on the Cross and pay the penalty for the sin of all of us – Muslims included. Jehovah loves you so much He made His

Son to be sin for you so you could be made righteous.[3] Allah hates mankind so much he demands all of us to send our sons to die for his benefit. Jehovah and Allah are polar opposites.

3. Jesus was raised from the grave and is alive and well. Mohammed still dead and in the grave. Mohammed was Allah's messenger, a mere man and not Allah's son. Mohammed is still dead because Allah, the God of Death, has no power or authority to raise him from the dead. Jesus, the Son of the Living God died, but His Father raised Him from the dead. Jesus is alive because His Father, the God of Life, has all power and authority over death to raise Jesus from the dead. And He did.

4. Jehovah is the God of Truth. Jehovah delights in keeping His Word, and He watches over it to perform it. Allah is the God of lies, he is capricious, doing and saying whatever he wants in order to serve his own desires. And he allows his followers to do the same. It's an Islamic principle called *taqiyya*.

Religious pluralism never works. You cannot reject every school of thought that results in disunity. Jesus is okay with division among people as long as it differentiates what is true from what is not true, the aim being to unite together on the side of truth.[4] Christianity was America's founding religion, the religion that made America great. The more we erode that foundation with religious pluralism, the less effective and weaker our nation grows. "A house divided against itself cannot stand."[5]

60 Days Praying for America

Journal - Personal notes, prayer points, & Scriptures you apply to this lesson.

Question: What do 1 Kings 18:21 and Colossians 2:8 have to say to those churches that condone reading the Quran during their services? Why does pluralism always fail? What are some other verses in the Bible that warn against mixing truth with falsehood?

_____

_____

_____

_____

_____

_____

_____

_____

_____

_____

_____

_____

_____

DAY 35

Entropy & Hall Closets

> "I now make it my earnest prayer that God would have you, and the State over which you preside, in His holy protection. That He would most graciously be pleased to dispose us all to do justice, to love mercy, and to demean ourselves with that charity, humility, and pacific temper of mind, which were the characteristics of the Divine Author of our blessed religion, and without a humble imitation of whose example in these things, we can never hope to be a happy nation."[2]

PERHAPS YOU'VE NOTICED that everything in your life needs constant attention and maintenance. Take your hall closet for instance. Go ahead, be brave. Open the door to your hall closet!

Whenever we open that door, we instantly notice that there is an information problem. More specifically, we find that every piece of information in the closet is mixed up with all the other pieces of information. Nothing is in order. Whatever it was we were looking for when we opened the door is difficult, if not nigh impossible to find. We are now forced to restore order just so we can find the piece of information we were looking for.

Restoring order means taking every piece of information out of the closet and determining its use and value. Then we must put all the pieces in order and determine the proper location each piece should occupy in the closet. Our chief problem with this process is that in one week's time we will open the door to the hall closet only to find disorder has returned. And until we repeat the process of restoring order to the hall closet again, the disorder will only grow worse.

That's the world we live in. Our world, our universe, is governed by the Second Law of Thermodynamics - entropy. Entropy is simply a scientific law stating that all things tend towards a state of disorder. If a rock rolls down a hill and hits a house, it's going to knock it into a pile of rubble. If a rock rolls down a hill and hits a pile of rubble, its' not going to knock it into a house. It's only going to knock it into a worse pile of rubble. If we want to decrease entropy and restore order, we've got to expend energy. We must expend energy to restore order in the hall closet.

It is the same with our nation. Maintaining the liberties of our nation depends on maintaining a proper government. The proper maintenance of our government depends on the virtue of its citizens. According to America's Founding Fathers, the best values for maintaining virtue are those found in the Bible.

Maintaining virtue is the responsibility of each citizen. Americans have cluttered their lives with pieces of information that conflict with biblical virtue. It is time for Americans to clean out the hall closet of their hearts. The more people in a nation fail to maintain their own virtue, the more coercive their government becomes, attempting to force them to maintain virtue. The more tyrannical the government, the greater the loss of liberty.

We will never understand the solution if we don't know what the problem is. Government cannot legislate enough laws to constrain or motivate people to live virtuously. That's because people do not have it in themselves to live virtuously, we need outside help. Not the help of government, but of God. That is why we must pray for ourselves and our nation. If God, the God of the Bible, will not help us, we will lose the will to live a virtuous life. Then government will become our overlord and our liberties will be lost.

How should we pray? Exactly as our founder's did:

60 Days Praying for America

"That He would most graciously be pleased to dispose us all to do justice, to love mercy, and to demean ourselves with that charity, humility, and pacific temper of mind, which were the characteristics of the Divine Author of our blessed religion, and without a humble imitation of whose example in these things, we can never hope to be a happy nation."

Journal - Personal notes, prayer points, & Scriptures you apply to this lesson.

Question: According to 2 Timothy 3:16, what is God's Word profitable for? What do "reproof", "correction", and "instruction in righteousness" mean? What instructions are found in God's Word that help you make adjustments to restore God's order in the "hall closet" of your life? In the "hall closet" of America's life?

_____

_____

_____

_____

_____

_____

_____

_____

_____

60 Days Praying for America

DAY 36

Let The River Flow!

> "... it is religion and morality alone, which can establish the principles upon which freedom can securely stand. The only foundation of a free Constitution is pure virtue, and if this cannot be inspired into our people in a greater measure, than they have it now, they may change their rulers and the forms of Government, but they will not obtain a lasting liberty."[1]

THERE IS NO FORM OF GOVERNMENT found in all the nations of men which can provide mankind with liberty. Liberty does not come from any government. Liberty begins in the heart of man. And if there is no liberty in a man's heart, then there is no government that may secure liberty for him.

Economy and jobs, any form of material security is only established in a nation when moral virtue and purity are established in men's hearts. The only means of establishing moral virtue and purity in a man's heart is through inculcating the biblical principles of Christianity. Liberty is a personal matter, not a governmental matter. People can fuss and muss all they want about the government not providing them with liberty. They are looking to the wrong source.

Pay close attention to what Jesus said: *... He has anointed me to proclaim good news to the poor. He has sent me to proclaim **liberty** to the captives and recovering of sight to the blind, to set at **liberty** those who are oppressed...*[2] Liberty begins and ends in a person's heart. Jesus is the Author and Finisher of liberty for all mankind. *If the Son sets you free, you shall be free indeed!*[3]

60 Days Praying for America

Liberty begins with Jesus, is released into the heart of the individual, and from there to the government of a nation. Just as water in a river never flows upstream, liberty never flows in reverse.

Even the Founding Fathers recognized this truth. George Washington called religion and morality the two "indispensable pillars" of America's government:

> "In vain would that man claim the tribute of patriotism who should labor to subvert these great pillars of human happiness… the mere politician equally with the pious man ought to respect an cherish them."[4]

In America today, too many have lost sight of this principle of liberty. We've tried to dam the river and reverse the flow by removing the Bible, prayer, and God's Law from schools, government, and society. And we've fairly well succeeded in damming the river. But we will never reverse the flow because no man and no government can provide liberty, only God can provide that.

There's no water that can be used to drain the swamp because the river's been dammed up. This is why conditions are stagnant in our government and society. It's time to let the river flow! Politicians and the government can't help. It's up to *you!* You're the only one who can seek the God of the Bible, gain His liberty, and let His river flow from your heart. The more Americans who do this, the more the swamp will be drained and liberty restored in our land.

> "Without morals a republic cannot subsist any length of time; therefore they who are decrying the Christian religion… are undermining the solid foundation of morals – the best security for the duration of free governments."[5]

60 Days Praying for America

Journal - Personal notes, prayer points, & Scriptures you apply to this lesson.

Question: How would you incorporate John 8:31-32, 36-36 into this lesson? How does freedom in a man's heart translate to freedom in government, society, and life?

DAY 37

Get Woke! ...or Caught Napping

> "When a Christian people feel themselves to be overtaken by a great public calamity, it becomes them to humble themselves under the dispensation of Divine Providence… to recognize His righteous government over the children of men, to acknowledge His goodness in time past, as well as their own unworthiness, and to supplicate His merciful protection for the future ..."[1]

IN THE NOT TOO DISTANT PAST, the better part of the first 150 to 200 years of America's history, most people in America humbled themselves under God's order and principles of righteousness. In the recent past, people in America have turned away from God, removing His Word and His standards of righteousness from schools, society, and government. The effects resulting from this change are causing a "great public calamity", a general agitation in America today. While this is a new situation in America, in most nations around the world the hostility caused by resistance towards Christianity is not.

The resistance we experience today against God, His Word, and His standards of righteousness is a general conflict that has existed throughout history. Psalm 2 talks about nations, kings, and leaders deliberating against the Lord and resisting His plan. God has put a plan in place to set Jesus Christ as King in Jerusalem. His plan is enforced by His covenants, specifically the Abrahamic, Land, Davidic, and Blood of Christ covenants, as well as His Law and His Word.

60 Days Praying for America

The Old Testament is replete with stories outlining how people and nations joined forces in an effort to resist God and His plan. As Israel followed the advice in the opening quote, humbled themselves and sought the Lord, they overcame the resistance.

America's Founders experienced this kind of resistance. The Founding Fathers had a firm understanding that the only thing securing the American form of government - a Constitutional-Republic - and the liberties secured by that government, is the moral character of each individual citizen. The Founders also understood that the best means of securing the morality of an individual is the promotion and teaching of biblical Christianity. As they followed the advice in the opening quote, they overcame the resistance and a nation was born which secured God-given liberty for each of its citizens.

Today, however, there are daily news articles retelling instances of prejudice against public expressions of Christian faith. Today's Christians must decide how they will face a situation very similar to that faced by Israel in the Old Testament and the disciples of the early church.

See if this sounds familiar: *They called them and commanded them not to speak at all nor teach in the name of Jesus.*[2] Today's news media is filled with reports of the same threats worldwide.

The disciples in the early church would have none of it. They followed the advice given in the opening quote, humbled themselves and sought God's intervention: *Now, Lord, look on their threats, and grant to Your servants that with all boldness* - with all outspokenness, with frankness and bluntness, publicly and with entire confidence - *we may speak Your word...*[3]

They weren't belligerent or obnoxious, they simply stood up and proclaimed God's truth. And they turned the world upside-down.

Christians today must choose to affirm, as the early disciples did, *Whether it is right in the sight of God to listen to you more than to God... For we cannot but speak the things which we have seen and heard.*[4] We must choose to humble ourselves under God, seek His righteousness and resolutely say, 'We will not be silent, but we will declare the Word of God with frankness and bluntness, with all outspokenness, publicly and in entire confidence. We must, lest we become like those who sleep and let their enemies in.[5]

Journal - Personal notes, prayer points, & Scriptures you apply to this lesson.

Question: Jesus gave stern warnings to His followers that they are not to be deceived. There are many Scripture verses that admonish Believers to be vigilant. Colossians 4:2; Proverbs 4:23; 1 Corinthians 10:12; and Matthew 26:41 are among them. What other verses do you know? By Scriptural standards, how vigilant are you? How vigilant is America?

_____

_____

_____

_____

_____

_____

_____

_____

_____

_____

DAY 38

Unprotected - Womb & Pulpit

> "Religion is of general and public concern and on its support depend, in great measure, the peace and good order of government, the safety and happiness of the people. By our form of government, the Christian religion is the established religion; and all sects and denominations of Christians are placed upon the same equal footing, and are equally entitled to protection in their religious liberty."[1]

WHOA! WHAT? America has an established religion?! And that religion is Christianity?! Well, we had an established religion, but it's no longer protected, it's unprotected. It's still present, behind the curtains as it were, but watered down, as evidenced by the United Methodist's decision to support abortion, in spite of biblical prohibitions against killing the unborn.[2]

Too many Christians and churches are conforming to principles of the world rather than to the principles of the Bible. As a result, the human fetus is no longer protected – in the womb or in the pulpit. If pulpits in churches are unwilling to stand up for the truth of God's Word and His protection of the life of the innocent, if church pulpits will not stand against abortion and the protection of innocent lives inside mother's wombs, why should those churches themselves be protected?

The more churches try to conform to the world's principles, the more unprotected those churches become. As a result, "the peace and good order of government, the safety and happiness of the people" declines.

60 Days Praying for America

Jesus never said that the gates of hell would not prevail against the church. What He said was, the gates of hell shall not prevail against the church built upon the Rock. Jesus also explained that a church builds on the Rock by obeying the Word of God.[3] Those churches that will not obey and stand on God's Word will be left unprotected. They will face failure.

The world always applies pressure and persecution to churches. Worldly pressure and persecution always destroy churches that are not built on the Rock. Those churches try to ease the pressure by twisting God's Word to conform to worldly standards. Churches that do this will cease to grow and will ultimately fail, just like a house built on sand.

Other churches will uphold the truth of God's Word and stand firm. Like a house built on Rock, they will continue to stand and experience growth. In churches built on the Rock, worldly pressure and persecution will always cause church growth. The stronger the attempts to bash and banish these churches, the more they thrive.

This is why "religion is of general and public concern and on its support depend, in great measure, the peace and good order of government, the safety and happiness of the people." This is why it is important for those churches and Christians who are built on the Rock to *go out and preached everywhere, the Lord working with them and confirming the word through the accompanying signs.*[4]

60 Days Praying for America

Journal - Personal notes, prayer points, & Scriptures you apply to this lesson.

Question: Protection. The apostle Paul talked about protection in Ephesians 6:10-18. Have you ever studied the Bible to learn how each piece of armor protects you? In 2 Corinthians 6:7 Paul talks about the armor of righteousness. How would failure to wear the armor of righteousness result in compromise with the world?

_____

_____

_____

_____

_____

_____

_____

_____

_____

_____

_____

_____

_____

DAY 39

Wasting Resources

> "Could many of our ills today have resulted from our failure to train a strong citizenry from the only source we have - the boys and girls of each community? Have they grown up to believe in politics without principle, pleasure without conscience, knowledge without effort, wealth without work, business without morality, science without humanity, worship without sacrifice?"[1]

WHAT MOST SCHOOL STUDENTS are currently being taught is this:

"Politics without principle" vote based on the color of a person's skin, on a person's gender, on their minority position, but never vote for a person based on their principles.

"Pleasure without conscience": 'if it feels good, do it'. No matter what "it" is and with no regard for the outcome.

"Knowledge without effort": to rely on electronic devices for answers – answers that are pre-determined for them - but never to think for themselves; the electronic devices will do your thinking for you.

"Wealth without work": many students still live with and are dependent upon their parents while their political leaders promise them a "universal basic income" for which they won't have to work; free money!

"Business without morality": Sun Tu's *Art of War* and Machiavelli's *The Prince* are taught in strategic management classes. They both teach that the

end justifies the means. This is quite different from principles of business as taught in the Bible.

"Science without humanity": it's called transhumanism. Not to worry, scientists will genetically alter you, robotically modify you, provide you with artificial intelligence to make you appear smarter than you really are, you'll be mostly disease free and live much longer, perhaps forever… yet still in your immoral state which scientists can do nothing to fix.

"Worship without sacrifice": even in church students are taught all that all you need to do is accept Jesus and you're good, He did everything for you, and you have no further responsibilities toward God.

Why do so "many of our ills today result from our failure to train a strong citizenry from the only source we have - the boys and girls of each community?" Oh, yeah. We removed prayer and teaching the Bible from our schools back in the early 1960s. A real stroke of genius.

Journal - Personal notes, prayer points, & Scriptures you apply to this lesson.

Question: What does Ezekiel 18:20 say about personal responsibility? Are you aware that the translators of the New International Version (NIV) of the Bible altered more than 2,000 personal pronouns from first person to the third person for the simple purpose of reducing your personal responsibility before God? What does Galatians 6:7-8 say about personal responsibility? Why is personal accountability at such a premium today?

_____

_____

_____

_____

60 Days Praying for America

60 Days Praying for America

DAY 40

Character Of A Generation

> "Now more than ever before, the people are responsible for the character of their Congress. If that body be ignorant, reckless and corrupt, it is because the people tolerate ignorance, recklessness, and corruption. If it be intelligent, brave and pure, it is because the people demand these high qualities to represent them in the national legislature… If the next centennial does not find us a great nation, it will be because those who represent the enterprise, the culture, and the morality of the nation do not aid in controlling the political forces."[1]

"THOSE WHO REPRESENT the enterprise, culture, and the morality of the nation."

- enterprise: corporate, business, and agriculture ventures which generate the commercial purpose of our nation.
- culture: society-at-large with all its ethnic and social interactions.
- morality of the nation: the moral character of each individual citizen.

If moral principle and character cannot be found in these three areas of our nation as a whole, how would we expect to find it in the halls of Congress? If moral principles and character are not taught in our school system or in our churches, how would we expect to find it in these three areas of our nation?

It's a trickle-down effect. Several generations ago our judicial system forced the teaching of biblical principles of morality out of our school systems. Students with little to no moral character entered into society and became

60 Days Praying for America

involved in various commercial businesses. The moral character of our nation's enterprises and culture steadily declined. And sure enough, individuals and corporations elect to office those who promote and protect their own selfish interests. Greed is not limited to corporate America; it is spread throughout society!

It's time to reverse the flow. America's school system and many of its churches won't teach biblical principles of morality. It is up to the individual, particularly those who are truly called by His name: Christ-ians.

In truth, the same challenge is faced by every generation. The disciples of the early church certainly faced it. Rather than succumb and live selfish lives as the world lives, they *denied themselves, took up their cross, and follow the Lord.*[2] True disciples abandon their own self-interests. True disciples get in the Word and discover the true value of righteous character. True disciples stand up and speak out for those same truths.

Journal - Personal notes, prayer points, & Scriptures you apply to this lesson.

Question: Read Matthew 16:24-25; 6:33; and Galatians 2:20. Whose interests do you stand up for and put first? How will you build your own character to fulfill these Scripture verses? How will this affect America?

_____

_____

_____

_____

_____

60 Days Praying for America

DAY 41

It's an Inside Job

> "We have men of science, too few men of God. We have grasped the mystery of the atom and rejected the Sermon on the Mount. Ours is a world of nuclear giants and ethical infants. The world has achieved brilliance without conscience. We know more about war than we know about peace, more about killing than we know about living. If we continue to develop our technology without wisdom or prudence, our servant may prove to be our executioner."[1]

WE LIVE IN A DAY AND AGE when a vast majority of people, especially those who appear to be 'in charge', believe that science will save mankind and grant us eternal life. The above quote was made by one of the generals who helped engineer the Allied victory in WWII. In lamenting man's propensity for war, he was also lamenting our turning away from biblical morality and turning towards science to answer our moral problems. This view is called scientism - a *belief* that the assumptions of scientific methods and research are equally appropriate and essential to all other disciplines (including religion).[2] Scientism has no basis of proof, it is a belief, a religion. And as stated above, it has replaced the principles of biblical morality.

There is a darkness lurking within mankind. Throughout history, men have repeatedly perpetrated unspeakable acts of cruelty and atrocities on other men. Whether it's those unspeakable acts history has recorded, or just the day-to-day selfishness all men express, there is a darkness lurking in all men. Have you ever noticed you don't have to teach children how behave badly?

They instinctively know how to behave badly. The question we all face is this: can mankind deliver itself from this darkness? Scientism says, 'Yes.' The Bible says, 'No.' To this point in history, the Bible has proved 100% correct.

Scientism, on the other hand, says the wickedness men do is caused by external forces - environment, upbringing, heredity, education (or lack thereof), or any other excuses they can come up with.

What is their answer for dealing with these outside forces that appear to be corrupting mankind? Science and technology will save us! Along with new laws, new systems of government, and new education systems to replace the old ones. In short, a New World Order which will eliminate all of those nasty external forces that cause men to be so evil.

The only thing strange about all that thinking is, that over the thousands of years of mankind's history, no state, no kingdom, no nation, no medical system, no educational system, no new technology, no new science, nothing man has ever implemented ever came close to delivering men from their evil nature. Not to worry, they say, we'll get it right this time. The problem we all face is inside of us, not outside.

For from within, out of the heart of men, proceed evil thoughts, adulteries, fornications, murders, thefts, covetousness, wickedness, deceit, lewdness, an evil eye, blasphemy, pride, foolishness. All these evil things come from within and defile a man.[3]

There is nothing wrong with good science, it has helped a lot of people. But, when science becomes a religion, it is totally incapable of solving the problem of mankind's evil nature. For America, and for that matter, all other nations, there is only one solution. The solution the Bible provides in Christ Jesus!

60 Days Praying for America

Journal - Personal notes, prayer points, & Scriptures you apply to this lesson.

Question: Scripture says we become the slave of whatever we present ourselves to – habits, ways of thinking, and so forth. Adam and Eve capitulated to the Serpent in the Garden, thereby surrendering all mankind to Satan's rule. Romans 8:7-8; Hebrews 2:14-15. Why do men look to anywhere but God for true freedom? Where do you look?

DAY 42

Read All About It!

> "[I am] disinclined to be longer buffeted in the public prints by a set of infamous scribblers."[1]

> "The man who reads nothing at all is better educated than the man who reads nothing but newspapers."[2]

> "I really look with commiseration over the great body of my fellow citizens, who, reading newspapers, live & die in the belief, that they have known something of what has been passing in the world in their time…"[3]

> "I am so accustomed to having everything reported erroneously that I have almost come to the point of believing nothing that I see in the newspapers."[4]

THESE ARE BUT A VERY FEW EXAMPLES. It seems even the Founding Fathers and past presidents – Democrat and Republican alike – were aware of fake news from the mainstream media of their days. Free Press? Hmm… Truth takes a beating for the sake of clickbait and pursuing personal agendas.

By covetousness they will exploit you with deceptive words…[5]

The time will come when they will not endure sound doctrine, but according to their own desires, because they have itching ears, they will heap up for themselves teachers; and they will turn their ears away from the Truth, and be turned aside to fables. But you be watchful in all things... [6]

God's Word is Truth.[7] To discern fake news from Truth, we must compare and contrast news bytes to the Word of God. Oh! Wait! That means we must read and study the Bible to be able to discern Truth from non-truth! But teaching the Bible and prayer have been removed from public school systems (and from most private schools and homes.) This means it is up to the individual Believer.

Be diligent to present yourself approved to God, a worker who does not need to be ashamed, rightly dividing the word of Truth. But shun profane and idle babblings, for they will increase to more ungodliness.[8]

Journal - Personal notes, prayer points, & Scriptures you apply to this lesson.

Question: What is the importance of comparing the values stated in the Bible with the values stated by news and entertainment outlets? Compare 2 Tmothy 3:16 with Hebrews 4:12. How would you use those two verses to live by the principles stated in 2 Timothy 2:15-16?

_____

_____

_____

_____

_____

_____

60 Days Praying for America

DAY 43

Genuinely Overcoming Stupidity

> "The word of the Bible that the fear of God is the beginning of wisdom[1] declares that the internal liberation of human beings to live the responsible life before God is the only genuine way to overcome stupidity."[1]

OH, WAIT! We've kicked God out of our education system. The vast majority of school children in America are not encouraged to fear the Lord, let alone seek Him. Does that mean we are raising stupid children? Well, consider this: the Federalist Papers, a series of eighty-five essays printed from 1787-88 and considered by some to be the primary documents of American history, were originally pamphlets that were passed out on street corners for the average citizen to read. Now they are considered graduate work in most colleges.

> "But these thoughts about stupidity also offer consolation in that they utterly forbid us to consider the majority of people to be stupid in every circumstance. It really will depend on whether those in power expect more from peoples' stupidity than from their inner independence and wisdom."[2]

America's Founding Fathers had it right. God, not the government, is the Author of individual rights – "inner independence and wisdom". Government's only duty is to secure those rights. So, let's see…

- God is the Author of individual rights.
- The fear of the Lord is the only genuine way to overcome stupidity.

60 Days Praying for America

- God and the Bible have been removed from our education system.
- Students are not learning the fear of the Lord, and therefore have no genuine way to overcome stupidity.
- With no genuine way to overcome stupidity, students have no understanding of their inner independence and freedom, nor of its True Source.
- With a nation of stupid citizens produced by our educational system, those in power can 'expect more from people's stupidity than from their inner independence and wisdom.'

All things that are exposed are made manifest by the light, for whatever makes manifest is light... the entrance of Your Word gives light.[3]

Lord, cause Your Word and Your light:

- to shine in Your Church and in the United States,
- to expose and remove misinformation, disorder, and lies, and to restore and increase Your information, Your order, and Your Truth.

Cause Your Holy Spirit-empowered Word to run swiftly and be glorified![4]

Restore the True Signal in the United States – restore the revelation that Jesus is the Christ![5]

60 Days Praying for America

Journal - Personal notes, prayer points, & Scriptures you apply to this lesson.

Question: Read Psalm 119:130-131 and explain how it applies to this lesson. In your opinion, why aren't Americans, or at least America's students who are forced to endure public education, living according to these verses?

_____

_____

_____

_____

_____

_____

_____

_____

_____

_____

_____

_____

_____

_____

DAY 44

Church Preserves

> "Had the people, during the Revolution, had any suspicion of any attempt to war against Christianity, that Revolution would have been strangled in its cradle... At the time of the adoption of the Constitution and the amendments, the universal sentiment was that Christianity should be encouraged, [but] not any one sect... In this age there can be no substitute for Christianity... That was the religion of the founders of the republic and they expected it to remain the religion of their descendants... The great vital and conservative element in our system is the belief of our people in the pure doctrines and divine truths of the gospel of Jesus Christ."[1]

"IN THIS AGE, there can be no substitute for the principles of Christianity."

Since there was no substitute in the days when independence was achieved during the American revolution, there can be no substitute now. The foremost problem Americans face today is that we are trying to substitute Christianity with any other code of conduct we can get our hands on. None of those substitutes will preserve our nation. As stated above, "Christianity was the religion of the founders of the republic and they expected it to remain the religion of their descendants... The great vital and conservative element in our system is the belief of our people in the pure doctrines and divine truths of the gospel of Jesus Christ."

What makes the doctrines of Christianity such a preservative? It is their immutability; they are changeless and timeless. God says what He means, and means what He says. And He never changes His mind. God's Word was true in biblical times, it was true in the days of America's founding, it is true today, and it will be true for all succeeding generations. *The grass withers, the flower fades, but the Word of our God stand forever.*[2]

Some people don't like what God says. That doesn't mean what He says is not true. The guy who wrote Proverbs put it this way, *Have I not written to you excellent things of counsels and knowledge, that I may make you know the certainty of the words of truth?*[3] God's Word contains excellent principles of counsel and knowledge. The fact that it cuts against the grain of some people's thinking doesn't make it any less true. All that means is that those people must make some adjustments in their thinking and actions in order to line up their lives with God's will. Only then will they find the peace and security they are looking for.

It is the same with any nation. How do the principles of Christianity preserve a nation? The same way they preserve an individual. We each must find out what God's Word says and live by it. *You are the salt of the earth; but if the salt loses its flavor, how shall it be seasoned? It is then good for nothing but to be thrown out and trampled underfoot by men.*[4] If America has enough individuals who are truly salted and seasoned with the Word of God, our nation will be preserved. If there are not enough individuals influencing secular society with the salt of God's Word, then not only our nation, but the individuals themselves, will be *good for nothing but to be thrown out and trampled underfoot by men.*

And who is responsible for the preservation process of individuals? Not the government. God forbid! Oh yeah. It's the church:

> "If immorality prevails in the land,
> the fault is ours [pulpit ministers] in a great degree.
>
> If there is a decay of conscience,
> **the pulpit is responsible for it.**

60 Days Praying for America

If the public press lacks moral discrimination,
the pulpit is responsible for it.

If the church is degenerate and worldly,
the pulpit is responsible for it.

If the world loses its interest in religion,
the pulpit is responsible for it.

If Satan rules in our halls of legislation,
the pulpit is responsible for it.

If our politics become so corrupt
that the very foundations of our government are ready to fall away,
the pulpit is responsible for it.

Let us not ignore this fact, my dear brethren;
but let us lay it to heart, and be thoroughly awake to our responsibility
in respect to the morals of this nation."[5]

Journal - Personal notes, prayer points, & Scriptures you apply to this lesson.

Question: Apply Psalm 119:11, Colossians 3:16, Acts 20:28, and 2 Timothy 4:2 to this lesson. Have you ever heard your pastor exhort, reprove, or rebuke concerning obedience to God's Word? How will you now begin to pray for your pastor?

_____

_____

_____

_____

_____

60 Days Praying for America

DAY 45

Counterfeit Character

> "Neither the wisest constitution nor the wisest laws will secure the liberty and happiness of a people whose manners are universally corrupt."[1]

HOW CAN YOU TELL the difference between God's Truth and the misrepresentations of His truth found in the world? Is it possible to tell if a person truly exemplifies biblical principles of morality by observing their lifestyle?

The answer to these questions requires some diligent effort: you yourself must get in God's Word, learn His Truths, and begin to live by them. Then, when you hear non-truths or half-truths, you'll recognize them as such because you are living the real Truth. As you observe a person's behavior, you can determine the level of their commitment to live by biblical truths.

It's the same method used to train federal agents to be able to instantly recognize counterfeit currency. Only allow them to handle and inspect the genuine article. Teach them to become completely familiar with real money so they can instantly spot a fake the moment they see and handle it.

Unfortunately, the ability to recognize God's Truth in our culture or in a person's lifestyle can be rather difficult these days. Studying the Bible used to be the core of American education. Today, the study of biblical principles is anathema in our educational system. The judicial verdicts of men have been allowed to overrule the truth of God's Word. We hear a lot said about "fake news" versus "real news." But it's the inability of people to distinguish true biblical character from "fake character" that lies at the root of issues facing our nation today.

Many would say that the Constitution is what rules America. But this is not so. America's is a representative form of government. America is ruled by the men and women we elect into office who are supposed to uphold the precepts of the Constitution. One of the delegates at the 1887 Constitutional Convention, John Mercer, put it this way:

> "It is a great mistake to suppose that the paper [the Constitution] we are to propose will govern the United States. It is the men whom it will bring into the government and the interest [they have] in maintaining it that are to govern them. The paper will only mark out the mode and the form. Men are the substance and must do the business."[2]

The ability and commitment of our elected officials to maintain the Constitution depends on their character – their moral character. If their character is of poor quality, how could we expect them to properly administer the Constitution's principles?

We are all affected by the decisions politicians make. You can moan and groan about those decisions and their effect upon you all you want, but you'll only end up living a long life of moaning and groaning. Prayer is much more effective. If you weren't praying for the right people to get into office before election day, you'd certainly better be praying for the ones who got elected.

> *When the righteous are in authority, the people rejoice;*
> *but when a wicked man rules, the people groan.*[3]
>
> *When the righteous rejoice, there is great glory;*
> *but when the wicked arise, men hide themselves.*[4]
>
> *When the wicked arise, men hide themselves;*
> *but when they fail and lose, the righteous increase.*[5]

60 Days Praying for America

*Let the wickedness of the wicked come to an end,
but establish the just.*[6]

Journal - Personal notes, prayer points, & Scriptures you apply to this lesson.

Question: The more you handle real money, the easier it is to recognize fake money. The more you live true biblical character, the easier it is to spot fake character. How does 1 John 1:1-4 apply to this principle? Could Proverbs 10:9 apply to a nation as well as an individual?

DAY 46

Gravity Works

> "The religion which has introduced civil liberty is the religion of Christ and His apostles, which enjoins humility, piety, and benevolence; which acknowledges in every person a brother, or a sister, and a citizen with equal rights. This is genuine Christianity, and to this we owe our free Constitutions of Government."[1]

WHOEVER HAS NO RULE over his own spirit is like a city broken down, without walls.[2] What happens to a city without walls? It is easily overrun, that's what happens. The same thing happens to anyone who has no rule over their own spirit. The same thing happens to a nation unable to rule its own spirit.

The flip side of the coin is this: Any city that has been broken down and overrun has been governed by men who are unable to rule their own spirit. Men who cannot rule their own spirit are unfit to rule a city, or to govern a state or a nation.

Why? Because those who cannot rule their own spirit will make decisions based on their own self-interest, whatever suits them at the moment. Thus, their decisions change from situation to situation. This trait of instability alone makes them unfit to rule a city or a nation.

If any country truly wants to establish civil liberties wherein all men are treated equally, there must be a set of rules and laws by which everyone abides. It would be most preferable for each individual citizen to personally govern their own affairs by the same set of rules and laws. Allowing individuals to make up their own rules will always lead to instability. It is then that a government will be required to create and enforce new rules and laws on its citizens. That would be nothing more than the tyranny we fought to escape during the Revolutionary War.

When America was founded, and for its first one hundred and fifty years or so, the rules and laws which people governed themselves by were the biblical principles of Christianity. Today, many in America have abandoned those principles and are looking for other rules to live by.

Because people claim to be "free" to choose whichever rules and laws they want, our society has begun to fragment. You have your truth, I have mine. Quit bugging me! When everyone attempts to govern themselves by different rules and laws, arguments and disagreements arise over varying opinions of right and wrong. Unfortunately, a house divided against itself cannot stand.

Are you one of those who says everyone should be able to do as they please and that we shouldn't judge people's actions and lifestyles? Then murder is okay, even if it's not your thing. Yesterday's crime is okay today, even though it's not your thing, because cultural norms have changed since yesterday.

We are attempting to live in a society where freedom is defined as being able to do whatever pleases you. A man claims to be a woman and vice versa. Why? Because he wants to, he likes it, it feels good to him. Self rules. That is not freedom. It is licentiousness – unrestrained selfish desire.

America's Founding Fathers understood that the degree to which all Americans govern themselves by principles of biblical Christianity will be the degree to which we will enjoy civil liberty. They understood that the degree to which Americans remove themselves from those principles is the degree to which we will lose our civil liberties and move towards the tyranny of government. They understood these things by experience. They had fought the battle to move from tyranny to civil liberty.

The events we are experiencing today are the opposite of our Founding Fathers. The more Americans violate the principles of biblical morality, the more they violate their own civil liberties. Americans are sliding from civil liberty to tyranny. Slides are easy because gravity works. It's the uphill battle our Founding Father's fought that we need to be engaged in.

Civil liberties are always founded and birthed in the biblical principles of Christianity. True civil liberty cannot be separated from true Christianity. Until the majority of Americans return to the principles of biblical morality and begin to rule their spirit by those principles, true liberty and civil rights will be at stake and in danger of being lost. Once they are lost, the government will step in to rule over the people, and tyranny will return.

Journal - Personal notes, prayer points, & Scriptures you apply to this lesson.

Question: Proverbs 14:12 talks about things that look good, but really are not. Galatians 4:9 talks about starting out strong in God and finishing weak… or not at all. How would you apply these verses to this lesson?

_____

_____

_____

_____

_____

_____

_____

60 Days Praying for America

DAY 47

Enslaved

> "The Christian religion was always recognized in the administration of the common law of the land, the fundamental principles of that religion must continue to be recognized in the same cases and to the same extent as formerly."[1]

Stand in the way and see,
and ask for the old paths, where the good way is, and walk in it;
then you will find rest for your souls.[2]

THESE TWO QUOTATIONS go hand-in-hand. The Bible verse urges us to pause everything we are doing for a moment, and then observe the difference between the way life used to be in America with the way life is now. For nearly the first two hundred years of America's existence, the principles of Christianity were part of the warp and woof, not just of America's culture, but also of its common law. Because of the inclusion of Christian principles, we were able to maintain our freedom and liberty. America was a strong nation.

But, over the last one hundred years or so, the principles of Christianity have been slowly removed from nearly every aspect of America's culture, government, and law, ultimately resulting in the decay of our liberties, freedom, and strength.

The way things stand today, most Americans confuse license for liberty. Under the attitude of license, a person can do whatever they want no matter if it's right or wrong; if it feels good, do it. And those who practice license don't want any interference from government, church, friends, neighbors, or anyone else in pursuit of their pleasures. That is not liberty, it is slavery.

Those who practice license are enslaved to the appetites of their pleasures. Alcoholics and drug addicts want to be "free" to get the next hit. Same for porn and sex addicts of any type. Same for money and power addicts. Whatever pleasurable pursuit it is that enslaves them is also draining the life out them – out of their self-respect, health, happiness, relationships, and finances. They will give up all of those things just to get the next hit, the next high. And they will lie, steal, and cheat to get it.

True liberty provides people the principles to live by wherein they can develop the strength to overcome and control the things that would enslave them. True liberty gives people the power to determine right from wrong and to live by what is right. The principles that allowed Americans to overcome the slavery of license, were the principles of Christianity. True liberty in America – freedom of speech, press, religion, and such notwithstanding - has been on the decline for quite some time. Most Americans today do not stand in liberty, they are slaves to their licentious pursuits.

So yes, it is time to stop and assess the principles in which we now stand, and compare them with the principles America stood on in the past.

"The Christian religion was always recognized in the administration of the common law of the land, the fundamental principles of that religion must continue to be recognized in the same cases and to the same extent as formerly… then we will find rest for our souls."

60 Days Praying for America

Journal - Personal notes, prayer points, & Scriptures you apply to this lesson.

Question: Luke 4:18; Galatians 5:1, 13 and James 1:25 all reference 'liberty.' Freedom is "the permission to do as you please." The problem with freedom is that it is granted by someone or something, it does not reside with the individual. According to these verses, are liberty and freedom the same thing? Which of the two would be more valuable?

_____

_____

_____

_____

_____

_____

_____

_____

_____

_____

_____

_____

_____

DAY 48

Your Nose Looks Funny

> "Our laws are found upon the Decalogue (Ten Commandments), not that every case can be decided by what is there enjoined, but we can never safely depart from this but great declaration of moral principles without founding the law upon sand instead of upon the eternal rock of justice and equity."[1]

> "A people unschooled about the sovereignty of God, the Ten Commandments, and the ethics of Jesus could never have evolved the Bill of Rights, the Declaration of Independence, and the Constitution. There is not one solitary fundamental principle of our democratic policy that did not stem directly from the basic moral concepts as embodied in the Decalogue and the ethics of Jesus."[2]

> "The moral principles and precepts contained in the Scriptures ought to form the basis of all our civil constitutions and laws. All the miseries and evils which men suffer from, vice, crime, ambition, injustice, oppression, slavery, and war, proceed from the despising or neglecting the precepts contained in the Bible."[3]

ACCORDING TO THE LIBRARY OF CONGRESS WEBSITE, the number of federal laws in force are uncountable. The United States Code contains 51 titles in multiple volumes, and that does not include case law and regulatory provisions. In 1982 the Justice Department tried to tally the total number of criminal laws. Over two years they drew up a list of about 3,000 laws. The whole project was an effort to get Congress to overhaul criminal code. The attempt failed.[4]

The first attempt to codify federal law in 1927 resulted in one volume. By the 1980s there were 50 volumes. As of 2016, IRS code contained about 3.4 million words and 7,500 pages. Usually, a new law means a new crime. From 2000 to 2007 Congress passed at least 452 new laws. Are you aware of all the laws you are obligated to abide by? There are so many laws it would seem impossible for everybody to not break at least one of them.

God made it much easier. He only had ten laws, which, if they were posted in every school, on all four corners of every intersection, and in every government building, would make our civil and municipal codes much easier to understand and follow. Everyone would know what laws they need to abide by, and would certainly know if they broke one of the ten.

Concerning those ten laws, John Quincy Adams said, "The law given from Sinai was a civil and municipal as well as a moral and religious code; it contained many statutes… of universal application – laws essential to the existence of men in society, and most of which, have been enacted by every nation which ever professed any code of laws."[5]

Alas, today rather than enact those civil and municipal codes, we repeal them in ignorance. Men will have none of it. We are convinced we know better: "A bill becomes unconstitutional, even though the wording may be constitutionally acceptable, if the legislator who introduced the bill had a religious activity in mind when he authored it.[6] This is little more than willful ignorance.

Of course, that court ruling would also preclude the Law of Love: *For all the law is fulfilled in one word, even in this: 'You shall love your neighbor as yourself. Love does no harm to a neighbor; therefore love is the fulfillment of the law.*[7] No, no, no! Too religious! And we all wonder why so many accusations of "that-phobic" and "this-phobic", and hater and hate-speech are hurled at people so often these days.

We have so many of man's laws when we only need ten of God's. In Indiana, it is illegal to catch a fish with your bare hands. In Mississippi it is legal, and it's called hand-grabbing. Beware! Due to all the AI and facial recognition software being installed and put to use at public places of transportation, a new law will undoubtedly soon be created requiring all citizens to get a nose job to make their face more recognizable.

Laws are made for the lawless. The problem is we are all lawless by nature. How many laws do people need to control themselves?

"All the miseries and evils which men suffer from, vice, crime, ambition, injustice, oppression, slavery, and war, proceed from the despising or neglecting the precepts contained in the Bible."[8]

Journal - Personal notes, prayer points, & Scriptures you apply to this lesson.

Question: Matthew 22:37-40. Why is all the law summed up in these two commandments? Why are men unable to conscientiously live by these two commandments?

_____

_____

_____

_____

_____

_____

60 Days Praying for America

DAY 49

Draining The Right Swamp

DURING AMERICA'S REVOLUTIONARY WAR the restraints of a government that was corrupt, unjust, and greedy, were replaced with a government that placed the rights and responsibilities of freedom on the individual instead of on the government itself.

But, before there was ever a Revolutionary War in America, there was another revolution which took place in the hearts and minds of men. This preceding revolution is referred to as the Great Awakening.

Before true freedom can be born in any government, it must first be born in the hearts of individual men and women. Reform in government cannot - and never will - occur until reform takes place in men's hearts. *Out of the heart proceed evil thoughts, murders, adulteries, fornications, thefts, false witness, blasphemies. These are the things which defile a man.*[1] Men can't be rehabilitated; they must undergo regeneration – they must be given a new heart. The Revolutionary War of 1776, which replaced governmental bondage with freedom, could never have taken place until men were released from the bondage in their hearts. What follows is one of many reports concerning the events of the Great Awakening.

> "In about a month or six weeks, there was a great alteration in the town, both as to the revivals of professors and awakenings of others. By the middle of December, a very considerable work of God appeared among those that were very young; and the revival of religion continued to increase; so that

in the spring an engagedness of spirit about things of religion was become very general among young people and children, and religious subjects almost wholly took up their conversation when they were together."[2]

And so it went from town to town. The Great Awakening directly affected two-thirds of the American population of that time.[3] What followed the revolution in their hearts was the revolution in their government. This is why William Penn said, *"Those people who will not be governed by God will be ruled by tyrants."* Until the swamp in men's heart is drained, the swamp in federal and state governments will never be drained.

We should be praying according to Isaiah 33:5-6,

- Lord, fill us with righteousness and justice.
- Lord, cause wisdom and knowledge and the strength of salvation to be the stability of our times.

Lord, cause the fear of the Lord to be our treasure!

Journal - Personal notes, prayer points, & Scriptures you apply to this lesson.

Question: Ezekiel 18:30-32; 36:26-27; Ephesians 4:22-24. Understanding the negative affects circumstances, society, and culture can have on a person or a government will not set anyone free. Why do men always think they can survive without God? Why should an individual take personal responsibility for their choices?

_____

_____

_____

_____

60 Days Praying for America

DAY 50

Dreams & Nightmares

> "I believe that the next half century will determine if we will advance the cause of Christian civilization or revert to the horrors of brutal paganism. The thought of modern industry in the hands of Christian charity is a dream worth dreaming. The thought of industry in the hands of paganism is a nightmare beyond imagining. The choice between the two is upon us."[1]

THIS STATEMENT was made in 1909. Sure enough, about fifty years later, the choice was made. Every attempt is being made to confine any mention of God within the four walls of the church. You can talk about the Bible and God in there, but not out in public. After all, faith is a private matter, keep it to yourself. By judicial decree, God and His Word and prayer were removed from our public schools, our rules of law and government, our media and entertainment, and so on.

Looking into the mirror of God's Word and comparing it with that decision, it is clear that the culture in America has become somewhat pagan. A person's destiny is no longer associated with their character. Our media and entertainment revels in adultery, abnormal sexual behavior, and violence. Abortion and infanticide are not just allowed, they are celebrated.

Underhanded dealings, where lying is approved as a means to justify the end result is practiced in both business and government. Alternative lifestyles of homosexuality, transgenderism, or simply changing partners for the sake of one's pleasure of the moment are the norm. Our news media works harder to form their listener's opinion than it does to inform their listeners. All that God calls evil and abhorrent is promoted and exported around the world. It's a nightmare.

So why pray? There is power in agreement. Many Christians are actively and fervently praying for America to once again line up with God's Word and His standards of righteousness. His Word points out the power of agreement:

Though one may be overpowered by another, two can withstand him. And a threefold cord is not quickly broken.[2]

I say to you that if two of you agree on earth concerning anything that they ask, it will be done for them by My Father in heaven. For where two or three are gathered together in My name, I am there in the midst of them.[3]

It's important to understand just how God's Word works:

All Scripture is given by inspiration of God, and is profitable for

- *doctrine-* which tells us what is right,
- *for reproof –* which tells us what is not right,
- *for correction-* which tells us how to get it right,
- *for instruction in righteousness –* which tells us how to keep it right,

that the man of God may be complete, thoroughly equipped for every good work.[4]

What is right; what is not right; how to get it right; how to keep it right. When praying for America, it is important not to pray just any old thing that pops into your head, but to pray God's Word. God's Word is precisely designed to clearly indicate what behaviors are right and what behaviors are not right. Once that distinction is made, God's Word will point out the corrections that need to be made, and it will provide instruction for maintaining a lifestyle of righteousness.

60 Days Praying for America

Judgment means to separate one thing from another. The primary purpose of God's judgment is to restore righteousness. God removes the nightmare so he can restore the dream. The American dream isn't free goodies and num-nums for all. The American dream is allowing everyone to exercise their God-given liberties under His rules of righteousness. That is what leads to happiness and prosperity.

The nightmare won't be reversed and the dream restored in the general population. It won't even happen in the church. It all starts by getting God's Word in *your* heart and fanning it into the flames of revival. Pray! And when you pray, pray his Word!

Journal - Personal notes, prayer points, & Scriptures you apply to this lesson.

Question: Read Daniel 1:17-20 and 1 John 2:15-17. Even though they lived in a pagan society, what enabled Daniel and his friends to remain separated from the influences of that society? According to 2 Timothy 3:16-17 what does God use to restore His order in an individual or in a society?

_____

_____

_____

_____

_____

_____

_____

60 Days Praying for America

DAY 51

Restoring Order in a Chaotic America

> "In this situation of this Assembly, groping as it were in the dark to find political truth, and scarce able to distinguish it when presented to us, how has it happened, sir, that we have not hitherto once thought of humbly applying to the Father of Lights to illuminate our understanding? …I therefore beg leave to move that henceforth prayers imploring the assistance of Heaven, and its blessings on our deliberations, be held in this Assembly every morning before we proceed to business."[1]

COMMUNICATION is a two-way street based on relationship. You talk while the other person listens. Then the other person talks while you listen. Prayer is simply a means of communicating with God. A wise person will let God do most of the talking. There are two aspects of prayer we should take into consideration as we pray for America.

First, all communication, including prayer, is based on relationship. Jesus Himself said, *This is eternal life, that they may know You* - by personal experience – *and Jesus Christ who You have sent.*[2] Some people complain that God is not near. Gnostics in particular claim that there is a God, but He is unknowable. That contradicts what Jesus said. God is always willing to talk *with* us. The question is, are we willing to listen to Him. Or do we spend all of our prayer time asking Him for stuff?

Is God speaking to us? Constantly. Then how do we hear Him? By reading His Word and letting Him use it to guide our life. *Hearing comes by the*

Word of God.[3] If you want to hear God speaking, you must read His Word. And, yes, just like any other relationship in your life, it takes a little time to establish the connection for effective communication.

We must also learn to pray according to His Word. God is the Creator of the universe. As such He is able (and willing) to put things in your life, and in the life of our nation, in order. In fact, if you carefully read His account of creation in Genesis chapter 1, you'll see that is exactly what He did. He took a chaotic world that was *without form and void*, and put everything back in order. And He used His spoken Word to accomplish that.

God's Word has the unique ability to expose and remove disorder, chaos, misinformation, and lies, and to restore and increase His order, His unity, His information, and His Truth. That's what God means when He says, *all things that are exposed are made manifest by the light, for whatever makes manifest is light. The entrance of* Your *Word gives light; it gives understanding to the simple.*[4] God even refers to His Word as a washing, cleansing agent.[5]

Therefore, it is important to find out what God says in His Word about the situations our nation faces, and to pray according to what He says, not what we think should happen. Praying in that manner will allow God to restore His order, His unity, His information, and His Truth, all of which we Americans desperately need. Undoubtedly, this is why prayer was called for more than 1,400 times in both colonial and federal government from 1620 to 1815.[6]

The Pilgrims and colonists came to America to escape tyrannical government powers that refused to let them pray and practice Christianity freely. It's astounding, but here we are in America today, under a tyrannical government that refuses to let people pray and practices Christianity freely!

It must be time for another revolution, a revolution of prayer. It is time to resist the tyranny of our own government and to begin praying in schools, in the halls of government, at sporting events, wherever and whenever we desire.

60 Days Praying for America

Not for show, not to garner attention, or to be annoying. Simply to exercise our right to practice Christianity freely.

As America stumbles in the dark trying to find political truth, the more important prayer becomes. Prayer allows God to restore His order. Ben Franklin couldn't have made a more important request.

Journal - Personal notes, prayer points, & Scriptures you apply to this lesson.

Question: Read Ephesians 5:13; Psalm 119:130. Besides these two Scriptures, what other verses can you find that support the concept that God's Word removes disorder and confusion, and restores His order? That God's Word confutes lies and establishes God's Truth?

_____

_____

_____

_____

_____

_____

_____

_____

_____

DAY 52

Absolutes Cannot Be Arbitrated

> "If we and our posterity shall be true to the Christian religion, if we and they shall live always in the fear of God, and shall respect His commandments, if we and they shall maintain just moral sentiments... we may have the highest hopes of the future fortunes of our country... It will go on prospering and to prosper. But, if we and our posterity reject religious instruction and authority, violate the rules of eternal justice, trifle with the injunctions of morality, and recklessly destroy the political constitution which holds us together, no man can tell how sudden a catastrophe may overwhelm us that shall bury all our glory in profound obscurity."[1]

WHY IS THIS STATEMENT CORRECT? What is it that provides stability in a people or a nation? What is it that causes instability in a people or a nation?

Today, truth is considered to be relative in any given situation. When you walk into a meeting room you must check your convictions at the door. It is the relationship, not your convictions, that must be maintained at all costs. Convictions will be negotiated until a mutual agreement is reached.

Today, truth can be manipulated and altered, it can be massaged to fit the purpose of the group currently in power. As circumstances change, truth can be further molded to help that group maintain power. However, after truth has been manipulated too many times, people should begin to ask what real truth is.

60 Days Praying for America

So, what is truth? A judge asked that question not too long ago during a case where the defendant faced capital punishment. The judge had decided many cases and was well acquainted with the shifting arguments of moral relativism, arguments where truth is manipulated to serve the purpose of one party over another. In this particular case, the plaintiffs had manipulated several laws of their own government to obtain their goal. The judge was wearied with the plaintiff's constantly changing evidence. "What is truth?", he asked in frustration. Surprisingly, it was the defendant who answered. "God's Word is Truth." The judge was Pilate and the defendant was Jesus. You're probably familiar with the outcome of the case. Moral relativism won again.

God's Word is absolute Truth. Absolute because there is no higher authority which can overrule the Word of God as written in the Bible. Absolute Truth will always provide stability. Manipulated truth will always be like sand, shifting from moment to moment.

America was founded and built on something that provided stability; the principles of Truth found in the Bible and Christianity. Since its founding, America has moved away from that foundation. It was Jesus who also said, *The wise man builds his house upon the Rock."* As I recall, He also said, *The foolish man builds his house upon the sand...* [2]

Absolute Truth never changes. It remains the same from situation to situation.

Journal - Personal notes, prayer points, & Scriptures you apply to this lesson.

Question: Read Matthew 7:24-27. What does a wise man build his house on? In the three verses preceding this passage (v. 21-23) how was Jesus discussing self-deception, and how do His comments apply to you? To America?

60 Days Praying for America

60 Days Praying for America

DAY 53

It Is What I Say It Is

> "We are not to attribute this prohibition of a national religious establishment to an indifference to religion in general, and especially to Christianity, which none could hold in more reverence than the framers of the Constitution."[1]

WHAT RELIGION DID THE FRAMERS of the Constitution hold in highest reverence? Oh, yeah, Christianity! All of the precepts and liberties secured in the Constitution of the United States are based on biblical principles of Christianity.

Did you know you can read the Constitution in about twenty-five minutes? Give it a shot some time, because unless you're my age you most likely never studied it in school. In the days after America's founding, the Constitution was read and taught in *elementary schools!*

Elementary students were required to recite catechisms and take written tests on the Constitution. These days the Constitution is so rarely read that the average citizen has no idea what his liberties are, let alone when they are being taken from him. These days, the Constitution is considered - falsely so! - to be so complicated that only judges and attorneys with the highest academic degrees can understand it.

In reality, the contents of the Constitution are so straightforward they can be considered barefaced. The Constitution is written so as to be easily understood. So were the Federalist Papers. They were printed from 1787 to 1788 as a series of pamphlets and newspaper articles explaining the

Constitution. They were written so the average citizen standing on a street corner or a farmer in town for the market could read and understand them.

Astonishing! Farmers, the average citizen, and elementary school kids could read the constitution and understand how government operates in the United States. But today the Constitution and Federalist Papers are taught only to upper-level academic highbrows. Why? Well, consider some of the following statements made by some of those highbrows:

> "The justification of a law for us cannot be found in the fact that our fathers always have followed it. It must be found in some help which the law brings toward reaching a social end."[2]

In other words, social agendas outweigh the truth; laws must follow society.

> "If there is any law which is back of the sovereignty of the state and superior thereto, it is not a law in such a sense as to concern the judge or lawyer."[3]

The basic intent here is that the laws of God as stated in the Bible are not to be considered as holding any higher authority over man-made laws.

> "I take judge-made law as one of the existing realities of life."[4]

Judges and attorneys do not want to be prohibited from making law. But the Constitution does just that, stating that judges are not elected to office and therefore only those elected *by the people* to serve in Congress can legislate laws. By elevating the teaching of the Constitution to the ranks of graduate-level courses, they keep you, the average citizen, from understanding the Constitution and from protesting when a judge overrules law as it is written in the Constitution.

Now you know why judges override Congress by judicial decision, deciding which laws Congress passes are 'Constitutional' or not. America's government is no longer representative. It is an oligarchy. We are ruled by

60 Days Praying for America

nine black-robed men and women who have declared, "We are under a Constitution – but the Constitution is what the judges say it is."[5]

Journal - Personal notes, prayer points, & Scriptures you apply to this lesson.

Question: Read Deuteronomy 16:18-20. What happens to a nation whose judges fail to deicide righteously according to God's law? What is the process in America for removing unrighteous judges?

_____

_____

_____

_____

_____

_____

_____

_____

_____

_____

_____

_____

DAY 54

On Its Ear

> "The people are the rightful masters of both Congress and the courts; not to overthrow the Constitution, but to overthrow those who would pervert it."[1]

IF MAN EVOLVED then laws must also evolve. The problem with that line of thinking is that man did not evolve. He was created. He was created by The Law Giver. And all men are held accountable for their compliance with the laws of the Law Giver.

"The people are the rightful masters of both Congress and the courts"

The God of the Bible is that Law Giver. Prior to the founding, at the founding, and for the nearly one hundred and fifty years after the founding of America's government and Constitution, it was clearly understood that God was the Law-Giver and that His authority was higher than any human authority. The Constitution was written with this principle at its core.

According to the Constitution, judges are excluded from having any role in making laws. Why? Because they are appointed to office, not elected. According to the Constitution, only elected officials can make laws because elected officials are held accountable to the people. Judges are appointed not elected. Therefore, because they are not accountable to the people, they are not allowed to make laws.

Today the Constitution has been set on its ear because judges legislate – make laws - from the bench according to their personal preferences and beliefs.

60 Days Praying for America

As a result, power has been removed from the hands of America's citizens and placed in the hands of unelected judges.

"To overthrow those who would pervert the Constitution"

At the outset of America's republican form of government, it was formally recognized that there were God-given standards for law and that all man-made laws were subject to God-given law. Our judicial system, as it functions today, is basically broken. As it stands today in America's judicial system, God is not the Law-Giver, man is. For the most part, our judicial system *regards God's law as broken and void*.[2] In America, a law is a law because the highest human authority – nine judges on the Supreme Court, the State – says so. And because the State has the force to back up what they say. This is why obtaining Senate approval for Supreme Court nominees is such a contentious process. Another of your liberties is lost.

In the long march of history unruly, men have always done their best to limit, inhibit, and prohibit the Word of God and His law. Why? Because they rebel against being held accountable to a Higher Authority. The early disciples faced this same challenge. Christian martyrs throughout history faced this same challenge. Yet being strong in the Lord, they withstood the evil of their day and took their stand.[3] Without arrogance or presumption, they were willing to simply declare that obedience to God supersedes obedience to human authority.

Journal - Personal notes, prayer points, & Scriptures you apply to this lesson.

Question: Read Romans 14:12 and Matthew 12:36-37. To who are all men ultimately accountable? In view of this, who should men obey first before anyone else?

60 Days Praying for America

DAY 55

Principle #7

> "The utopian dreams of leveling (equal distribution of goods) and a community of goods (central ownership of the means of production and distribution) are as visionary and impractical as those which vest all property in the crown. These ideas are arbitrary, despotic, and in our government, unconstitutional."[1]

THE PILGRIMS who arrived at plymouth rock first attempted a system of socialism – the common ownership of labor and of land. Share and share-alike. Within two years their economic socialism failed so miserably that they came to the same conclusions mentioned in the quote above: socialism is as impractical as vesting all property in the crown (State), and the concept is arbitrary and despotic.

William Bradford, governor of Plymouth Colony, provided a written record of why the pilgrims quickly changed from a system of socialism to a free market economy. In his record, he outlines six principles for a free market system:[2]

1. Common ownership of labor and land causes people to become lazy and unwilling to work. Private property generates a free and more productive economy.

2. In socialism, people make excuses for being unable to work (much like they do under a welfare system). Therefore, private profit generates a free and more productive economy.

3. Under socialism, everybody wants what everyone else has but they are not willing to work for it. Discontent reigns. Providing a welfare system -charity - must be voluntary and not coerced by the State.

4. Because socialism is based in pride and a supposed 'equality' among all, it opposes God's plan as outlined in the Bible. Differences between the young, adults, and the aged are not respected. (Those who are unproductive, a status produced by socialism itself, are deemed unnecessary and eliminated.) A free economy is built on the respect and dignity of individual differences.

5. While some consider the profit motive to be corrupt, it is important to understand the reality that it is man's nature that is corrupt, even among those holding an office in government (if the State controls the economy, it will do so with no less corruption, and usually more, than the individual citizen.) The free market is built on personal incentive and self-interest precisely for the purpose of allowing the individual the opportunity to defeat their naturally corrupt nature.

6. God's economy depends on voluntary choice (consider Ananias and Saphira) as being much more productive than the government for redistributing wealth.

Thomas Jefferson put it this way:

"To take from one, because it is thought that his own industry and that of his fathers has acquired too much, in order to spare to others, who, or whose fathers have not exercised equal industry and skill, is to violate arbitrarily the first principle of association, 'the guarantee to every one of a free exercise of his industry, and the fruits acquired by it."[3]

When the pilgrims abandoned an economic system of socialism and adopted a free market economy, the result was an immediate tripling of any previous

60 Days Praying for America

production! Governor Bradford also mentioned a seventh principle that is required for a successful free economy:

PRAYER!

Journal - Personal notes, prayer points, & Scriptures you apply to this lesson.

Question: Read Proverbs 12:24; 13:4; 21:25-26 and 2 Thessalonians 3:10. If the government giveth, then the government can taketh away. Who is responsible to make provision for the poor, governments or individuals? According to these Scriptures under what form of government will people be most able to make provision for the poor?

_____

_____

_____

_____

_____

_____

_____

_____

_____

_____

DAY 56

Indispensable Alliances

> "My own private judgment has long been - and every day's experience more and more confirms me in it - that government cannot long exist without an alliance with religion; and that Christianity is indispensable to the true interests and solid foundations of free government."[1]

WHY WOULD a former U.S. Supreme Court chief Justice publicly declare that government cannot long exist without an alliance with religion, and as specifically pointed out, the Christian religion? That's not what Supreme Court justices are saying these days!

At one time, America had deep spiritual roots embedded in Christianity. The charters of the original colonies were steeped in affirmations of biblical faith. Those statements were reaffirmed in the Declaration of Independence, and out of those affirmations of biblical faith came the inalienable rights written in the Constitution. It's not that those statements of biblical faith were forced upon America's citizens. No, that decision was left up to the conscience of the individual.

Yet it was firmly understood that those rights outlined in the Constitution are God-given rights. Those rights are not something the Founding Father's got together and came to some kind of consensus on. The Source of those rights is firmly grounded in the God of the Bible. And those rights are secured by His Law as outlined in the Bible.

60 Days Praying for America

Furthermore, the Founding Fathers understood that since the inalienable rights stated in the Constitution are God-given and secured by His Law as outlined in His Word, then the laws by which we as a people choose to govern ourselves must be subject to His Law.

In the hearts and minds of the Founding Fathers, a government separated from religion, specifically the Christian religion, would soon be overthrown. And while it was not acceptable to them to establish Christianity or any one denomination of Christianity as the state-approved religion, it was their highest desire that Christianity should be supported and protected in the educational and judicial systems as a means of establishing a moral society and a sound government.

During the first one hundred and fifty years of America's history, the alliance between our government and Christianity was secure. That is a fact proven in historical documents and court rulings. However, over the last one hundred years, that alliance has been slowly, steadily dissolved. Teaching the Bible and prayer have been removed from the educational system. And according to a U.S. Supreme Court Chief justice: The Constitution "must draw its meaning from the evolving standards of decency that mark the progress of a maturing society." In other words, the civil laws that govern us are no longer subject to the higher standard of God's Law, they are now subject to 'standards of decency' as determined by society. Who said society was maturing?!

If America is to have any hope of getting back on its feet, there must be a strengthening of the bonds of the alliance between government and Christianity, which is *indispensable to the true interests and solid foundations of free government*." Our civil laws must once again be subject to God's Law and education must include the basic principles of Christianity.

It's time for Christians to quit standing around with their hands in their pockets. If government leaders and judges will not resolve this issue adequately, then it is up to us to raise our children with a godly, biblical education.

Journal - Personal notes, prayer points, & Scriptures you apply to this lesson.

Question: Read Proverbs 14:34; 28:4, 28; and 29:2, 18. Referencing these Scripture verses, how would you apply responsibility and accountability to the individual? To the government?

_____

_____

_____

_____

_____

_____

_____

_____

_____

_____

_____

_____

DAY 57

Revolution Against Tyranny

> "Had it not been the purpose of God that His will should be done on earth as it is done in heaven, He would not have commanded us to pray for it. That command implies a prediction and a promise that in due season it shall be accomplished."[1]

FROM 1620 TO 1815, between the colonial, state, and federal governments there were over 1,400 official calls to prayer.[2] Let's see, that's 195 years, at twelve months per year… if I've done the math correctly, that averages out to one official call to prayer every 50 days or so. Once every fifty days for one hundred and ninety-five years, America's leaders and founders prayed corporately! That doesn't include the individual prayers all of them prayed in-between those fifty days. Clearly, from America's earliest days through its founding, prayer was extremely important to the Founding Fathers and to the populace as well.

The speaker in the quote above is referring to what is commonly called' The Lord's Prayer', the prayer Jesus taught His disciples to pray:
When you pray, say: 'Our Father in heaven, hallowed be Your name. Your kingdom come. <u>Your will be done on earth as it is in heaven</u>. Give us day by day our daily bread. And forgive us our sins, for we also forgive everyone who is indebted to us. And do not lead us into temptation, but deliver us from the evil one.'[3]

60 Days Praying for America

> "Had it not been the purpose of God that His will should be done on earth as it is done in heaven, He would not have commanded us to pray for it."

Prayer is a spiritual discipline. Prayer is more than just the recitation of words. Prayer is the turning of the heart of an individual, the heart of a nation, to commit to learning and doing the will of God as written in His Bible. An individual commits to this and goes about doing so on a daily basis. The more individuals in a nation that commit themselves to praying and obeying, the more secure that nation is. America and its people need prayer as much now as they did then, if not more so.

Hands down, it was the spiritual discipline of prayer during the early days of American history that helped in the founding of this nation. A revolution of prayer is needed today for God's will, not man's will, to be done in America. Prayer is a God-given right. Yet tyrants "devise evil by law"[4] attempting to prevent prayer in the halls of schools, government, or nearly anywhere else in public.

Wanna join the revolution? PRAY!

Journal - Personal notes, prayer points, & Scriptures you apply to this lesson.

Question: James 5:16 indicates that the prayer that avails much is effectual. In this verse, the phrase "effectual fervent" is expressed using only one Greek word: *energeo*. *Energeo* means active and efficient. In your own honest assessment, how active are you in praying for America? What are two things you could do to increase your effectiveness in prayer?

_____

_____

_____

60 Days Praying for America

DAY 58

Restoration: Love Where You Live

> "Neither the wisest constitution nor the wisest laws will secure the liberty and happiness of a people whose manners are universally corrupt."[1]

GOD IS IN THE RESTORATION BUSINESS. Obviously, He doesn't lack for opportunities. He is constantly called upon to *Restore us, O God; cause Your face to shine, and we shall be saved!*[2] God is fully capable of restoring His order by means of supernatural power. But His primary method of restoration is done by providing the information contained in His Word – the Bible. When applied in a person's life, the truths contained in the information of the Bible will remove disorder, chaos, and lies. At the same time, they will restore God's order, unity, and truth. As people commit themselves to obey those truths, God is able to work through them to restore His order amidst the chaos of the world. In this manner, God prefers that we become *workers together with Him.*[3]

God's restoration and the liberties it produces are always an inside job. God's process of restoration always works from the inside out, never from the outside in. Liberty begins in the heart of man, not in the external constitutions and laws that govern a man. The only true source of liberty that governed the manners of an individual are the truths found in the Word of God.

60 Days Praying for America

Whittaker Chambers was a spy for Soviet Russia for many years before disavowing his allegiance to communism. He later stated that his main reason for abandoning communism was his realization that freedom begins inside a man's heart.

> "Freedom is a need of the soul, and nothing else. It is in striving toward God that the soul strives continually after the condition of freedom. God alone is the inciter and guarantor of freedom. He is the only guarantor. External freedom is only an aspect of interior freedom. Political freedom, as the Western world has known it, is only a political reading of the Bible."[4]

If Americans want their liberties restored, they would do well to follow the advice of Samuel Adams in the opening quote and amend their manners according to God's Word. As Samuel pointed out, the wisest constitution and the wisest laws are incapable of amending people's manners. Only by obeying the Word of God can a person restore corrupt manners. George Washington agreed with Samuel Adams when he said,

> "Of all the dispositions and habits which lead to political prosperity, religion and morality are indispensable supports."[5]

Thousands of years of human history have proved mankind's inability to rule our moral behavior according to God's Word. But in all those thousands of years, God has kept His restoration business up and running. We just need to call on Him:

If My people who are called by My name will humble themselves, and pray and seek My face, and turn from their wicked ways, then I will hear from heaven, and will forgive their sin and restore their land.[6]

60 Days Praying for America

Journal - Personal notes, prayer points, & Scriptures you apply to this lesson.

Question: Read John 17:3. It is one thing to be restored by the Lord. It is entirely another thing to have a personal relationship with the Lord. What do Ephesians 1:17-18 and James 1:22-25 have to say about this. How does removing Bible teaching and prayer from schools apply to this lesson?

_____

_____

_____

_____

_____

_____

_____

_____

_____

_____

_____

_____

_____

DAY 59

Truth or Consequences

> "Upon my arrival in the United States the religious aspect of the country was the first thing that struck my attention; and the longer I stayed there, the more I perceived the great political consequences resulting from this new state of things, to which I was unaccustomed. In France, I had almost always seen the spirit of religion and the spirit of freedom marching in opposite directions. But in America, I found they were intimately united and that they reigned in common over the same country."[1]

THE *"POLITICAL CONSEQUENCES"* that resulted from the *"religious aspect of the country"*. Imagine that. There are political consequences that must be faced due to the religious attitude of a nation. In America that religion is Christianity and no other. If the attitude of the institutions and policies of our nation are strong towards Christianity, then the nation and our liberties are stable, strong, and prosperous.

Not long ago a study was done by political scientists attempting to determine the origin of the political thinking of the Founding Fathers. They examined over 15,000 papers from the time period of America's founding, 1760-1805. Identifying 3,154 quotes, they found the most cited source was the Bible. Scriptures were quoted over four times more frequently than the next most cited source.[2]

This agrees precisely with the opening quote: "In America the spirit of religion [Christianity] and the spirit of freedom were intimately united and that they reigned in common over the same country." There was no 'separation of church and state.' The author of the opening quote also said, "politics and religion contracted an alliance which has never been broken."

Until now. The more vigorously our leaders apply the counterfactual argument of 'separation of church and state', the more our liberties erode away.

> "The Christian religion is the most important and one of the first things in which all children under a free government ought to be instructed… No truth is more evident to my mind than that the Christian religion must be the basis of any government intended to secure the rights and privileges of a free people. Education is useless without the Bible"[3]

"No truth is more evident… than that the Christian religion must be the basis of any government intended to secure the rights and privileges of a free people." Why is this?

Because liberties are God-given. They are found in the hearts of men, not in the hands of a government. Therefore, if the people of any nation want to be free, they must learn to rule themselves inwardly. If the people of any nation are unwilling or unable to rule themselves inwardly, then the government of that nation will need to apply laws, regulations and force to keep the people under control. The more laws and force any government requires in order to keep its citizens restrained in word and in action, the less freedom those citizens have and the more liberty they lose.

The central problem facing the Founding Fathers was two-fold: 1) creating a government for the primary purpose of securing the liberty of those governed, 2) providing a means for those governed to rule themselves individually so the government will not have to rule over them.

The first step, creating the proper government, was the easier part. But how to provide the proper means for individual people to rule themselves inwardly and to maintain a proper moral character? For if the people are not able to do that, the government would have to do it for them.

The Founding Fathers came to the conclusion that the best means of accomplishing this is by the application of the moral principles of Christianity in the lives of individual citizens. Those principles of morality *were and are*, the only and most effective means for a person to rule over the avarice of their own human nature and self-interests.

In contrast today, America's government and courts have decided that it is illegal to teach the Bible or even to pray in America's educational system. Or pretty much anywhere in government or any public setting. In arrogance and self-pride, they have removed *the first thing* all children should be taught, they have removed the "basis of our government intended to secure the rights and privileges of a free people."

Once God has been kicked out, can the loss of God-given rights be far behind? No. And that is what we see taking place daily in America, the erosion of our God-given liberty because we refuse to personally govern ourselves by the moral principles of the Bible.

Journal - Personal notes, prayer points, & Scriptures you apply to this lesson.

Question: How would you apply Proverbs 3:5-6 to this lesson? Verse 6 can more accurately be translated, *In all your recurring opportunities acknowledge Him, and He shall direct your paths*. What recurring opportunities do you have to apply this principle in your life? What recurring opportunities does America have to apply this principle?

_____

_____

_____

60 Days Praying for America

DAY 60

Now You Know How

> "If religious books are not widely circulated among the masses in this country, I do not know what is going to become of us as a nation. If truth be not diffused, error will be; If God and His Word are not known and received, the devil and his works will gain the ascendancy. If the evangelical volume does not reach every hamlet, the pages of a corrupt and licentious literature will; If the power of the Gospel is not felt throughout the length and breadth of the land, anarchy and misrule, degradation and misery, corruption and darkness will reign without mitigation or end."[1]

THE STATED PURPOSE of the Communist Party in America is to contaminate the country's educational system by:

- Eliminating prayer or any phase of religious expression in the schools on the ground that it violates the principle of 'separation of church and state'.

- Discrediting the Bible and emphasize the need for intellectual maturity which does not need a 'religious crutch'.

- Controlling schools, using them as transmission belts for socialism and current Communist propaganda.

- Soften curriculums, get control of the teacher's associations.

- Put the party line in textbooks... control student newspapers..."[2]

John Adams considered Benjamin Rush, George Washington, and Benjamin Franklin to be the three most notable figures among America's Founding

60 Days Praying for America

Fathers. Benjamin Rush was a distinguished doctor in Philadelphia and was often referred to as "The Father of American Medicine." He was also a signer the Declaration of Independence. Taking a stand against slavery, Rush helped start America's first abolition society. Recognized as an educator, he helped start the nation's first Bible society as well as five colleges, and he wrote several textbooks. He was considered "The Father of Public Schools Under the Constitution."

At the present stage in the history of our nation, we may do well to reconsider the advice of those who helped to establish our educational system. Benjamin Rush, along with the other Founding Fathers, did not *recommend* that the Bible be used as a textbook, they *insisted* that it be used as a textbook in America's school system. In an essay written in 1791, Rush listed five reasons for "preferring the Bible as a school book to all other compositions…:

1. That Christianity is the only true and perfect religion; and that in proportion as mankind adopt its principles and obey its precepts, they will be wise and happy.

2. That a better knowledge of this religion is to be acquired by reading the Bible than in any other way.

3. That the Bible contains more knowledge necessary to man in his present state than any other book in the world.

4. That knowledge is most durable and religious instruction most useful when imparted early in life.

5. That the Bible when not read in schools is seldom read in any subsequent period of life.[3]

To reprise the opening quote: "If the power of the Gospel is not felt throughout the length and breadth of the land, anarchy and misrule, degradation and misery, corruption and darkness will reign without mitigation or end."

Mitigation: to lessen the force and intensity of something unpleasant, such as wrath, pain, grief, or extreme circumstances.

Take a look at the corporate and political leadership in America. Take a look at the behavior of people in the public square. What do you see? Do you see any anarchy, misrule, degradation, misery, corruption, or darkness? Now you know why. The reason you are seeing these things is because the power and influence of the Gospel is not at work in those people, in those institutions, nor in those situations.

Our Founding Fathers were exceptionally wise in their insistence that the Bible be the primary text in education. Those who oppose the use of the Bible in education are either extremely ignorant or deliberately subversive.

Would you like to know how to mitigate the effects of anarchy, misrule, degradation, misery, corruption, and darkness in the corporate and political leadership in America and in the behavior of society-at-large? Now you know how. Get the Bible and its teachings back in the educational system.

Journal - Personal notes, prayer points, & Scriptures you apply to this lesson.

Question: Romans 8:5-8, 13 presents the effects of two opposing lifestyles. Galatians 5:16-26 tells us how to live the correct lifestyle. So, how are you doing? How is America doing? What can you do better? What can America do better?

_____

_____

_____

60 Days Praying for America

Addendum A: Voting & Elections

PRAYER PREPPER'S CALL TO ACTION PART 1

THE PURPOSE OF PRAYER isn't so much to get needs met as it is to get direction from God.

God, I need a new car. God, I need a new job. God, my marriage is in trouble. God, my kids are in trouble. God, I need... God, I've got troubles. Help me, God!

God isn't moved by our needs; He is moved by our faith. God is moved by our faith in Him and in His Word. We prove our faith in God by changing our lifestyle to line up with His Word.

When God performed His work of creation in Genesis chapter 1, He looked out over an earth that was '*without form and void.*'[1] He was looking at an earth that was a total mess. Nothing was in order, none of the pieces were properly fitted together, it was completely uninhabitable. As Isaiah 45:18 says, *For thus says the LORD Who created the heavens; God himself that formed the earth and made it; He hath established it, He created it not in vain* - without form confused, a waste place - *He formed it to be inhabited.*

So, God began His task of fitting all the pieces together, getting His order and His unity restored, and making earth habitable again. It was a six-day process. On day one, He removed a little bit of the disorder and chaos, and restored a little of His order and unity. He did the same on days two through six, removing a little more disorder and chaos while restoring a little more of His order and unity each day. Finally, at the end of day six, He had achieved

Addendums

a perfect self-sustaining world. It remained that way until Adam and Eve blew it.

Here is what is critical for us to notice in all of this. God restored His order and unity through the use of His Word. Every time He spoke, the world was restored to increasing order. The power contained in His Word has the ability to do that. That is the power and the process noted by the centurion who asked Jesus to come and heal his servant, *Only speak a Word and my servant will be healed.*[2] Jesus marveled at the centurion's faith in God's Word.

God is not moved by our needs. God is moved by our faith in Him and in His Word.

That is how prayer works in our individual challenges, and in the challenges of our nation! Prayer is two-way communication. We ask God a question and then we listen to His answer from His Word. We get direction from His Word on how to resolve the challenges the way He wants them resolved. And if we need to change the way we think and live our life differently so it lines up with His Word, then we make those changes. We make those changes according to His Word so we can achieve the results HE desires - His order, His unity, His Truth – in our lives. And in our nation! That process is called repentance. Repentance is good for an individual and for a nation!

Our nation goes through an election cycle every couple of years. Your state and your community also go through election cycles. At the beginning of each cycle, not at the end, all of us should prepare to pray! We should spend a little time each day in God's Word and find out what God says about nations. What does God expect and demand from nations, from their leaders, and from their citizens?

Ask the Holy Spirit to help you learn. As He points out different verses write them down along with a few notes. Then, when you pray for the elections you will have gotten some direction from God on what His will and desire is for nations. Pray according to those Scriptures and you'll be praying in

Addendum A: Voting & Elections

agreement with His will. You'll be praying with His power! Here are a few verses to help you get started:

Leviticus. 18:24-25 Deut. 11:22-23; 12:2; 28:1, 12
2 Kings 17:33, 41 1 Chronicles 16:24, 31
2 Chronicles 20:5-12 Ezra 6:21
Colossians 1:13-14 Malachi 1:11

Psalms. 22:7; 33:9-12; 46:10; 66:7; 67:1-4; 86:9-10; 96:3, 10; 98:2

Reader! Whoever you are, remember This!

Do not put your trust in princes,
nor in a so of man, in whom there is no help.
His spirit departs, he returns to his earth;
in that very day his plans perish.[3]

The Donkey and the Elephant can't help anyone.
It's time to return to the Lamb!

Lord, turn Your hand upon us,
and purely purge away our dross,
and take away all our mixture,
... restore our judges as at the first,
and our counselors as at the beginning.
Then wisdom and knowledge
shall be the stability of our times,
and strength of salvation:
the fear of the LORD is our treasure.[4]

We make our prayer before the LORD our God,
that we might turn from our iniquities
and understand Your truth.[5]

Addendums

Turn the people to the Lord their God,
turn the hearts of the fathers to the children,
turn the disobedient to the wisdom of the just...
make ready a people prepared for the Lord.[6]

Addendum A: Voting & Elections

PRAYER PREPPER'S CALL TO ACTION PART 2

DURING HIS DEALINGS WITH MANKIND, God made several covenants with men and with nations. Most of these covenants were implemented in part to repair and restore man's partnership with Him in ruling over His creation. Some Bible teachers refer to these covenants as the backbone of the Bible story. Understanding God's covenants not only helps us see the big picture presented in the Bible, it also helps us understand the smaller details of the biblical story.

Many of God's covenants with men are conditional. If men will do this, then God will do that. 2 Chronicles 7:14 is a good example. God tells Solomon that whenever the nation of Israel finds itself in trouble, if those people in the nation who are called by His name will do four things – humble themselves, pray, seek His face, and turn from their sin, then God will do three things - hear from heaven, forgive their sin, and heal their land. The fulfillment of this covenant is conditional on the response of the people who are called by God's name. If they will fulfill their part of the covenant, then God will fulfill His part. We'll come back to this in a moment.

Of all the covenants God made with men, there are four in particular that are eternal and unconditional. That these covenants are eternal simply means they will be enforced as long as there is an earth; they cannot be rescinded. That these covenants are unconditional simply means they are one-sided covenants. The only party with any responsibility to fulfill the terms of these covenants is God. God's fulfillment of these covenants is independent of

Addendums

mankind's actions, good or bad. Man has no part, except to receive or refuse the benefits of these covenants. In brief, here are those four eternal and unconditional covenants, and why they will bear important considerations as we pray for America and upcoming elections:

Abrahamic Covenant: given in Genesis 12, contains seven 'I will's':

1. I will make of you a great nation,
2. I will bless you,
3. I will make your name great,
4. I will make you a blessing,
5. I will bless them that bless you,
6. I will curse him that curses you,
7. In you, I will bless all families of the earth.

Today, this covenant is contested by the world. There are many who say God has withheld judgment from America because America is Israel's closest ally and supporter. For this reason alone, America cannot afford to turn its back on Israel.

Land Covenant: stated in Genesis 15. God promises to give Abraham and his descendants – the nation of Israel – all the land *from the river of Egypt to the great river, the River Euphrates.* (The next time someone mentions the West Bank, ask them which river they're talking about.) Today, this covenant is contested by all the Arab nations. America is one of the few nations supporting Israel's right to be in the land.

Davidic Covenant: Stated in 2 Samuel 7:11-16 and re-affirmed in Luke 1:32, it refers to return of the Lord Jesus Christ to rule and reign on Earth, establishing God's covenants, God's Law, God's Word, and the Kingdom of Heaven on earth. Today, this covenant is contested by, of all things, denominational churches which claim that the church has replaced Israel in God's plan. Nothing could be further from the truth!

Addendum A: Voting & Elections

Blood of Christ Covenant: As stated all throughout the Old and New Testament, this refers to the restoration of man's relationship with God, and man's rulership and dominion in God's Kingdom. This restoration was achieved through the death and resurrection of Jesus Christ. This restoration is available to anyone who will receive it. America has been one of the nation's primarily responsible for the spread of the Gospel of Christ around the world.

Concerning these covenants and elections, when you vote, have you determined the candidate

- that best supports these principles?
- that supports the law and the Constitution?
- that best supports and promotes biblical values?

You can vote for the candidate you think might give you the greatest monetary gain and the most government handouts. But consider this: prosperity follows righteousness, righteousness does not follow prosperity. In fact, *"the love of money is the root of all evil."*[1] So, it's very clear what will follow those who vote for the candidate they think will give them the most financial gain, over the candidate who best supports Biblical principles and the Gospel of Jesus Christ.

Elections will soon be held around our nation. Prepare to Pray! Start *now!* As mentioned above in 2 Chronicles 7:14, God says, *If My people who are called by My name...* This covenant with its promises doesn't apply so much to praying for a nation as it does for those in any nation who are truly called by the name of God, 'Christ'-ians, to pray and seek God themselves. Those who do not bear the name of God will not pray. Many people who have taken on the name of God for self-serving purposes, vanity Christians, will not pray. But, if true Christians will do those four things God lists in these verses, then God will most certainly fulfill the three things He promised.

Addendums

One of the church's primary responsibilities is working together with God in supporting and promoting these four covenants. It will be important to include these covenants in our prayers.

Reader! Whoever you are, remember This!

Do not put your trust in princes,
nor in a so of man, in whom there is no help.
His spirit departs, he returns to his earth;
in that very day his plans perish.[2]

The Donkey and the Elephant can't help anyone.
It's time to return to the Lamb!

Lord, turn Your hand upon us,
and purely purge away our dross,
and take away all our mixture,
... restore our judges as at the first,
and our counselors as at the beginning.
Then wisdom and knowledge
shall be the stability of our times,
and strength of salvation:
the fear of the LORD is our treasure.[3]

We make our prayer before the LORD our God,
that we might turn from our iniquities
and understand Your truth.[4]

Turn the people to the Lord their God,
turn the hearts of the fathers to the children,
turn the disobedient to the wisdom of the just...
make ready a people prepared for the Lord.[5]

Addendum A: Voting & Elections

PRAYER PREPPER'S CALL TO ACTION PART 3

AS THE LITTLE GIRL LAID DOWN TO SLEEP, her father asked her what she would like to pray about. "Onions", the girl replied. So, they prayed about onions. The next morning the Dad asked his daughter why she wanted to pray about onions. "Because," she said, "the pastor told us we should pray for things we don't like."

When it comes to prayer, preparation is the key to success! What are you prepared to pray about concerning America? Onions?

In the Declaration of Independence, after listing the ways in which the British government restricted their liberties and freedoms, America's Founding Fathers appealed "to the Supreme Judge of the world for the rectitude [rightness of principle] of our intentions…" In the current elections, all those in America who lay claim to being called by the name of the God of the Bible, 'Christ'-ian', will have the opportunity to appeal to the same "Judge of the world."

Will God judge America?

When will God judge America? Some ask that question enthusiastically as if they are eagerly waiting for God to reduce America to a pile of rubble so they can rebuild it the way they want it. They misunderstand the purpose of God's judgment. They view it as a punishment resulting in total destruction. From a biblical perspective, this is not judgment.

Addendums

The term judgment means 'to separate.' I don't like red M&M's. If I open a package of M&M's and toss out all the red ones and eat the rest, I have judged the red M&M's. I separated out the red ones. When God judges a person, organization, or nation His first purpose is to remove – to separate out – what is evil from what is good according to His standards of righteousness (not according to their standards!) What makes that judgment seem so hard to some people is that their desire is for the evil, not for the good.[1]

The second purpose in God's judgments is redemption. He separates out what is evil so He can restore His order and His righteousness. The purpose of God's judgment is not punishment and destruction. The purpose of all God's judgment is redemption, the restoring of His order and His righteousness in the life of a person, organization, or nation. God's judgment is a form of discipline to encourage us to follow after His righteousness and His holiness. *Judgment will return to righteousness, and all the upright in heart will follow it.*[2]

What can a remnant do?

Many say that America is a post-Christian nation, and there is much evidence in favor of that argument. However, a closer look reveals the following:[3]

- Since 2007, the number of people claiming to be Christian declined by 8%, from 78% to 70%. So, yes, there is a decline in those claiming to be Christian.
- Membership in mainline denominational churches has declined by 5 million since 2007. This decline has occurred primarily because these churches have taken to mimicking the world, accepting homosexuality, abortion, free sex, the belief that Allah and the God of the Bible are the same, and so forth. All the while rejecting the truths of the Bible: there is a heaven and a hell, Satan and sin are both real, salvation is in Christ alone.

Addendum A: Voting & Elections

- Yet during the same timeline, membership in evangelical churches increased by 5 million. Huh! I wonder where all those people came from? People are leaving the polluted teachings of denominational churches in favor of more accurate biblical teachings of evangelical churches.

A remnant is merely something that is left over. In the eyes of the world, the remnant of Christianity in America is worthless. Yet, God has done astounding things with a remnant of righteous people.

If Abraham could have found ten righteous people in Sodom and Gomorrah, God would have spared those cities. But Abraham couldn't find ten righteous.[4] I know at least ten righteous in America, and they are praying…

Should we pray for God to judge America?

The revolution we now fight is a revolution to regain and restore biblical Christian principles in the Church, in the public arena, in schools, in government and politics, in media and in the news, in the courts, and in society at-large.

"We appeal to the Supreme Judge of the world" to separate out from our nation, whatever stands in the way and prevents us from meeting His standards of righteousness, and to restore His redemption in America.

Reader! Whoever you are, remember This!

Do not put your trust in princes,
nor in a so of man, in whom there is no help.
His spirit departs, he returns to his earth;
in that very day his plans perish.[5]

The Donkey and the Elephant can't help anyone.
It's time to return to the Lamb!

Prepare to pray for America's elections! Start *now!*

Addendums

Lord, turn Your hand upon us,
and purely purge away our dross,
and take away all our mixture,
... restore our judges as at the first,
and our counselors as at the beginning.
Then wisdom and knowledge
shall be the stability of our times,
and strength of salvation:
the fear of the LORD is our treasure.[6]

We make our prayer before the LORD our God,
that we might turn from our iniquities
and understand Your truth.[7]

Turn the people to the Lord their God,
turn the hearts of the fathers to the children,
turn the disobedient to the wisdom of the just...
make ready a people prepared for the Lord.[8]

Addendum A: Voting & Elections

ELECTION DAY

Truest Friend

SOME FRIENDS WERE PLAYING A GAME of hide and seek, but the game went on for hours. Good friends are hard to find.

We often refer to mere acquaintances as 'my friend so-and-so.' We collect 'friends' on social media like baseball cards. What's plainly obvious is that 'friends' come and go. Is there some kind of friendship that is truer and richer than what our technology burdened society offers today? Beyond personal relationships, can there be true friends of a nation or true friends of liberty?

> "He therefore is the truest friend to the liberty of this country who tries most to promote its virtue, and who, so far as his power and influence extend, will not suffer a man to be chosen into any office of power and trust who is not a wise and virtuous man....The sum of all is, if we would most truly enjoy this gift of Heaven, let us become a virtuous people."[2]

"*A friend loves at all times, and a brother is born for adversity.*"[1] How can you tell who is a true friend?

Liberty is a gift of heaven. All the Founding Fathers of America recognized liberty as a God-given right, not a construct of man's decisions. In order to enjoy this gift of heaven, the people of any nation *must* be virtuous. Benjamin Rush, a signer of the Declaration of Independence, put it more succinctly, "…without virtue there can be no liberty…"[3]

Every four years America gets involved in an election cycle that is finalized during general elections in November. During these election cycles, much is said about various economic plans, social issues, and conditions around the

Addendums

world. However, not much is said about biblical virtue as it pertains to securing the God-given liberty established at America's beginnings. Or, if statements are made about biblical principles, they are twisted for the purpose garnering votes and gaining political power.

So, how does a Christian determine how to vote? Republican? Democrat? Libertarian?

You shall not take the name of the LORD your God in vain, for the LORD will not hold him guiltless who takes His name in vain.[4] Originally, mankind was created in the image of God, but we blew it early on and lost the ability to image God's character and nature. It was God's grace and mercy through Jesus' death and resurrection that made a way for us to regain the ability to be His imagers.

"Christ"-ians are to properly exhibit the name "Christ" and to be examples of His character and nature. Of course, there are always a few who are Christian in name only, they in no way exemplify the character and nature of Jesus. Just as there are RINO and DINO politicians, there are CINO's, Christian In Name Only, or vanity Christians.

What does this all have to do with voting in an election? Who should Christians vote for? Republican? Democrat? Libertarian? Actually, none of these. As Christians, we are called to be monarchists. We are to be ambassadors of the Coming King. Do you call yourself a Christian, yet you still vote for worldly values? Or are you truly committed to being an ambassador for the Coming King?

Many candidates lay claim to the Christian religion. But once in office, they exemplify and pursue policies that are not based on biblical principles of morality. With the lack of biblical teaching in our educational system, it becomes the responsibility of the individual Christian to dig into the Word of God, learn its principles of morality and righteousness, and live them as a true

Addendum A: Voting & Elections

imager of Christ. Only then will we be able to vote into "any office of power and trust a person who is a wise and virtuous man."

Pray first. Then vote.

It's an operating principle the founders of America staked the future of the nation on:

> "He therefore is the truest friend to the liberty of this country who tries most to promote its virtue… The sum of all is, if we would most truly enjoy this gift of Heaven, let us become a virtuous people."

> "If we abide by the principles taught in the Bible, our country will go on prospering and to prosper; but if we and our posterity neglect its instruction and authority, no man can tell how sudden a catastrophe may overwhelm us and bury all our glory in profound obscurity."[5]

Reader! Whoever you are, remember This!

Do not put your trust in princes,
nor in a son of man, in whom there is no help.
His spirit departs, he returns to his earth;
in that very day his plans perish.[5]

The Donkey and the Elephant can't help anyone.
It's time to return to the Lamb!

Addendums

Addendum B: Thanksgiving Day

THANKSGIVING DAY

Are You A Pilgrim?

"pilgrim": an alien alongside; a resident foreigner.

IN A NUTSHELL, a pilgrim is a stranger in a foreign land. The apostles Peter and Paul referred to Christians as "pilgrims":

Peter, an apostle of Jesus Christ, to the <u>pilgrims</u> of the Dispersion in Pontus, Galatia, Cappadocia, Asia, and Bithynia… and it is just as easy to say "the pilgrims in America!"[1]

In the Bible, and in God's view, a pilgrim is a person who represents God and the truth of His Word in a world that does not agree with His biblical standards of righteousness.

Are you a pilgrim?

As examples of God's true pilgrims, Paul mentions Abel, Enoch, Noah, Abraham and Sarah, Isaac, Jacob, Joseph, Moses, Rahab the harlot, Gideon, Barak, Samson, Jephthah, David, and Samuel. Paul goes on to say that there are many others he doesn't have time to name.

Paul finally says, *These all died in <u>faith</u>, not having received the promises, but having seen them afar off were assured of them, embraced them and confessed that they were strangers and <u>pilgrims</u> on the earth.*[2] You can read what Paul says about them in Hebrews chapter 11. You can find their full stories in the Old Testament.

What made these men and women pilgrims?

Addendums

They believed God says what He means and means what He says. And they ordered their lives according to what God told them. That is what faith is – believing God says what He means and means what He says, and living by it.

Are you a pilgrim?

Peter gave us a couple of hints about how God's pilgrims are to live: *Beloved, I beg you as sojourners and <u>pilgrims</u>*

1. *... abstain from fleshly lusts which war against the soul,*
2. *having your conduct honorable among the Gentiles, that when they speak against you as evildoers, they may, by your good works which they observe, glorify God in the day of visitation.*[3]

Paul also told us how a pilgrim of God is to live while in an alien world: *I beseech you therefore, brethren, by the mercies of God,*

1. *that you present your bodies a living sacrifice, holy, acceptable to God, which is your reasonable service.*
2. *And do not be conformed to this world and its pop culture,*
3. *but be transformed by the renewing of your mind, that you may prove what is that good and acceptable and perfect will of God.*[4]

Are you a pilgrim?

God's name is Jehovah. It is usually translated as "Lord", but it means so much more. Jehovah means "the always existing one Who makes Himself known." Or, more accurately, "the Lord Who reveals Himself unceasingly!" God unceasingly reveals Himself to you in the hope that you will pursue a genuine relationship with Him. The question is, are you listening?

God reveals Himself through His Word. Paul told us that His Word is profitable to those who wish to be His pilgrims, who wish to have a real relationship with Him: *All Scripture is given by inspiration of God, and is profitable for*

Addendum B: Thanksgiving Day

- *doctrine* – which tells us what is right,
- *reproof* – which tells us what is not right,
- *correction* – which tells us how to get it right,
- *instruction in righteousness* – which tells us how to keep it right,

that the <u>pilgrim</u> of God may be complete, thoroughly equipped for every good work. Are you reading God's Word a little each day and making adjustments to line up your life with what He says?

Are you God's pilgrim?

Four hundred years ago, in 1620, pilgrims came to America. They came to America because they were not free to worship and obey God in the other nations they lived in. The world always resists and argues against God and His Word. True pilgrims always live their life according to God's Word.

Those pilgrims established colonial governments that allowed people the freedom to worship and obey God – the God of the Bible, not just any god – as they deemed proper according to His Word. Ultimately, they founded an entire nation based upon those same principles.

Freedom never comes from a government. No government can secure liberty for its people. Freedom comes from God and it begins in the heart of man: *For out of the heart proceed evil thoughts, murders, adulteries, fornications, thefts, false witness, blasphemies. These are the things which defile a man.*[5] We are enslaved by our own human nature, not by any outside forces or circumstances. *If you abide in My word, you are My disciples indeed. And you shall know the truth, and the truth shall make you free* – from the slavery of your own human nature.[5]

Americans are only "free" when they obey God. If we do not obey God, then the government must pass more and more laws to control our unruly human nature. The more laws the government must pass, the more liberties we lose and the more we find ourselves once again under the oppression of tyranny.

Addendums

Are you a pilgrim?

Pilgrims left their homeland to better serve God in a foreign land. Those of us who are truly born-again are supposed to be pilgrims in this world – a foreign land. As such, even though we endure trials as America's pilgrims did, we should still abound with thanksgiving.

… while you are enriched in everything for all liberality, which causes thanksgiving through us to God.[7]

Today, America does not need social justice warriors, moral relativism, or tolerance. All of which have little or nothing to do with God's Word and His standards of righteousness. Today, America needs all the pilgrims and prayers it can get! America needs pilgrims who like the disciples of the early church prayed, *Now, Lord, look on their threats, and grant to Your servants that with all boldness* - with all out-spokenness, with frankness and bluntness, publicly and with entire confidence – *we may speak Your word, by stretching out Your hand to heal, and that signs and wonders may be done through the name of Your holy Servant Jesus.*[8]

America needs pilgrims who will pray as Daniel did: *All this disaster has come upon us; therefore we make our prayer before the LORD our God, that we might turn from our iniquities and understand Your truth.*

Are you a pilgrim?

Addendum C: Scriptures

SCRIPTURES

I WANT TO PRAY FOR AMERICA, but how should I pray? Why doesn't this devotional provide prayers I can pray each day? What is the best way to pray for America, or for any nation for that matter?

You may rightly ask, why are there no "template" prayers at the end of each day's devotional. Well, for just that reason, they would be "template" prayers. They would be someone else's prayers, not your prayers. Prayer, true prayer, is based on relationship. All relationships require communication, and prayer is based on communication – good communication.

Jesus clearly stated that eternal life, God-Life, is knowing God on a personal basis. Eternal God-Life requires that our relationship with the God of the Bible is based on personal experience. God does not want us to know "about" Him, He wants us to know Him personally. He wants us to walk, talk, and live with Him. That is precisely what Jesus said, *This is eternal life, that they may know You, the only true God, and Jesus Christ whom You have sent.*[1] That word "*know*" is the Greek word *ginosko*, and it means to know someone by personal experience. As a publisher, *Ginosko House* desires to encourage people in their pursuit of knowing God and His Son Jesus on a personal basis. For this reason, no pattern prayers are provided with the devotionals.

As you read each day's devotional, my open and heartfelt prayer is that you will develop your own personal relationship with the Living God – Jesus Christ. That you will begin to know Him through these devotionals so you can talk with Him yourself. Why use my prayers, or someone else's prayers,

Addendums

that are based on our relationship with God, but not your relationship. *You get to know Him.*

Prayer, communication with God, is a two-way street. God talks and you listen, then you talk and God listens. How does God talk to you? Through His Word. God clearly states in His Bible that there is information – communication – to be gained by hearing what God says in His Word. *All Scripture is God-breathed and is profitable for*

- *Doctrine:* which tells us what is right,
- *Reproof:* which tells us what is not right,
- *Correction:* which tells us how to get it right,
- *Instruction:* which tells us how to keep it right,

that the man of God may be complete, thoroughly equipped for every good work.[2]

You may remember this being mentioned in a couple of the devotionals. In His Word, God tells us what His desires and plans are for the nations (and for you!). He tells us what He thinks of the actions and plans that nations take, and how He will respond to those actions and plans. God says a lot about nations in the Bible.

With that in mind, if we understand God's thinking and plans for nations, then we will know how to pray in agreement with Him. The best way to pray for nations, or anything else, is to pray using His Word. Find out what God says about nations and situations and pray in agreement with what He says. The prayer of agreement is not getting together with someone else and asking God to agree with our plans. The prayer of agreement is finding out what God says and getting in agreement with Him. The more people there are who are praying in agreement with God, the more powerful their prayers.

What follows is a list of Scriptures you can use to begin to learn what God says about nations, all nations, not just America. Ask the Holy Spirit to guide

Addendum C: Scriptures

and teach you according to the lessons in these verses. He will. If you have questions, ask Him. Better yet write down your questions, then write down the answers He gives you from His Word. Be patient while waiting to hear what He will say to you.

There is no one right way to pray. Give yourself to learning what God has to say regarding nations and then pray accordingly. These are but a few Bible verses to get you started. There are many more waiting to be found by the diligent.

> *If My people who are called by My name will humble themselves, and pray and seek My face, and turn from their wicked ways, then I will hear from heaven, and will forgive their sin and heal their land.*
>
> 2 Chronicles 7:14

The righteous contrasted with the wicked:

Psalm 1:4, 6; 7:9-10; 10:2; 66:7-8; 94:20; 119:126
Proverbs 10:11; 12:5; 20:7; 25:5; 28:1, 4, 12, 28; 29:18
Romans 1:18
1 Peter 3:10-12

Cleansing & cleaning:

Hebrews 9:13; 12:29;
Ephesians 5:11-14, 26-27
2 Thessalonians 3:1-3
1 John 3:3

Nations:

Leviticus 18:24-25
Deuteronomy 18:9, 14; 28:1
2 Kings 17:33, 41
1 Chronicles 16:24, 31

Addendums

Ezra 6:21
Nehemiah 5:9
Psalm 9:15-20; 22:28; 33:10-12; 46:10; 67:1-4; 86:9-10; 96:10; 98:2
Zechariah 2:11; 8:22
Revelation 2:26; 7:9

These are just a few verses about God's dealings with the nations. They should serve to get you started and make you just a little bit more curious to dig into His Word and learn more. But one of the best verses on how God deals with nations is this:

So when they heard that, they raised their voice to God with one accord and said: "Lord, You are God, who made heaven and earth and the sea, and all that is in them, who by the mouth of Your servant David have said:

> *Why do the nations rage,*
> *And the people plot vain things?*
> *The kings of the earth take their stand,*
> *And the rulers are gathered together*
> *Against the LORD and against His Christ.'*

For truly against Your holy Servant Jesus, whom You anointed, both Herod and Pontius Pilate, with the nations and the people of Israel, were gathered together to do whatever Your hand and Your purpose determined before to be done. Now, Lord, look on their threats, and grant to Your servants that with all boldness they may speak Your word, by stretching out Your hand to heal, and that signs and wonders may be done through the name of Your holy Servant Jesus.[3]

This is the prayer the disciples prayed after the leaders of the Jews told them to quit preaching the name of Jesus or face the consequence. Does this sound familiar to events taking place today? The world and its ruler are always

Addendum C: Scriptures

trying to subjugate the Word of God to their purposes. They will never succeed.[4]

The disciples faced a situation where various worldly leaders and "nations" were agreeing together do, ... not their plans, but *whatever God's Hand and purpose determined before to be done*. Ironic isn't it? The nations and their leaders plot, plan, and devise schemes to resist and overthrow God, His covenants, and His Word. And they never succeed. God always accomplishes His plans and purposes.[5]

It's also interesting that God affected His plans and purposes when His people prayed. The disciples prayed. Then God went to work. And it wasn't long before rulers began crying out, *These who have turned the world upside down have come here too!*[6]

The effective, fervent prayer of a righteous man avails much.[7] It is time to turn America, or whatever nation you live in, and the world upside down one more time! Get in God's Word and pray!

Addendums

End Notes

A Note From The Author

1. Luke 1:16-17
2. Daniel 9:13
3. Isaiah 1:25-26; 33:6
4. Matthew 7:17-20
5. Jeremiah 20:9; 23:29
6. Henry, Patrick, in a hand-written message on the back of an original copy of the 1765 Stamp Act Resolutions passed by the Virginia legislature and included in his will, 1799.
7. Ibid.
8. John 17:17
9. John 8:31-32
10. Psalm 146:3-4
11. Daniel 9:13
12. Isaiah 1:25-26; 33:5-6
13. Luke 1:16-17

Day 1

1. Wilson, Woodrow, 28th President of the United States, *The Road Away From Revolution*, The Atlantic Monthly, Aug. 1923.
2. Roosevelt, Franklin, 32nd President of the United States, in a speech at the Dedication of the Great Smoky Mountain National Park, Sep. 2, 1940.
3. Proverbs 14:34
4. John Adams, 2nd President of the United States, *The Works of John Adams*, ed. Charles Francis Adams, Little, Brown and Company, Boston, MA, 1850, Vol. X, pp. 45-46, to Thomas Jefferson, Jun. 28, 1813.
5. 1 Timothy 2:1-4
6. Motto of Giuseppe Mazzini, propagandist and founder of Italy's secret revolutionary society, Young Italy, 1832.
7. 2 Chronicles 7:14

Addendums

8. Psalm 94:10-13

Day 2

1. Noah Webster, *The History of the United States*, New Haven: Dury and Peck, 1833, p. 309.
2. Wallace v. Jaffree, 1984.
3. Exodus 20:7
4. Matthew 5:13-20
5. John 17:14-17
6. Acts 4:19-20

Day 3

1. Rev. Witherspoon, John, the Works of the Rev. John Witherspoon, Philadelphia: William Woodard, 1802, Vol. 111, p. 46.
2. Psalm 33;12; 144:15; Jeremiah 17:7-8
3. Exodus 20:7
4. 1 Peter 1:15-16
5. Ephesians 6:12
6. James 5:16
7. Acts 4:29; Ephesians 6:19
8. Matthew 16:24

Day 4

1. Adams, Samuel, Speech at the State House of Pennsylvania, Philadelphia, Aug. 1, 1776.
2. Sparks, Jared, *The Library of American Biography, Vol. II,* p. 318, "The Life and Adventures of Captain John Smith, by George S. Hillard, New York, Harper and Brothers, 1846.
3. 2 Thessalonians 3:10
4. Franklin, Benjamin, *The Works of Benjamin Franklin,* ed. Jared Sparks, Vol. II, pp. 445-446.

End Notes

Day 5

1. Cuomo, Chris, CNN News Anchor, interviewing Alabama Supreme Court Justice Roy Moore, Feb. 13, 2015.
2. Eisenhower, Dwight D., 34th President of the United States, *"Remarks for the 'Back-to-God Program' of the American Legion"*, Feb. 20, 1955.
3. Webster, Noah, History of the United States, New Haven, CT, Durrie & Peck, 1832, p. 6, Preface.

Day 6

1. Bonhoeffer, Dietrich, *Letter and Papers From Prison*, p. 9, 1951.
2. Proverbs 26:4-5
3. Psalm 14:1
4. Washington, George, 1st President of the United States, *Farewell Address*, 1796.
5. James 4:6, 8
6. Prov 28:1
7. 2 Timothy 3:16-17

Day 7

1. Webster, Daniel, U.S. Secretary of State, in a speech to the City Council of Boston, MA, May 22, 1852.
2. Washington, George, 1st President of the United States, "A Proclamation", printed in *The Providence Gazette and Country Journal*, Oct. 17, 1789.
3. Matthew 16:17-18
4. John 14:6
5. Matt 7:24, 26
6. Psalm 119:126 Romans 1:18; Psalm 94:20; Proverbs 28:4

Day 8

1. Madison, James, *The Papers of James Madison,* ed. Henry D. Gilpin, Vol. III, p. 1324, John Francis Mercer, delegate of the Constitutional Convention, Aug. 14, 1787.
2. Proverbs 29:2

Addendums

3. *collections of the New York Historical Society for the Year 1821*, Vol. III, pp. 32, 34, "An Inaugural Discourse Delivered Before the New York Historical Society by the Honorable Gouverneur Morris (President), Sep. 4, 1816."

Day 9

1. *People v. Ruggles*, 1811, Chief Justice James Kent, New York Supreme Court.
2. John 8:31-32
3. Luke 6:43-45

Day 10

1. Coolidge, Calvin, 30th President of the United States, at the Unveiling of the Equestrian Statue of Francis Asbury, First American Bishop of the Methodist Episcopal Church, Oct. 15, 1924.
2. Penn, William, *Some Fruits of Solitude*, 1682.

Day 11

1. Jedidiah Morse, *A Sermon Exhibiting the Present Dangers and Consequent Duties of the Citizens of the United States of America, Delivered at Charlestown,* April 25, 1799, *the Day of the National Fast*, Charlestown, MA, printed by Samuel Etheridge, 1799, p.11.
2. John 14:6
3. Ephesians 5:13-14; Psalm 119:130
4. Ps 2:10-12

Day 12

1. Nardi, William, *Professors call Founding Fathers 'terrorists,' founding ideals a 'fabrication'*, The College Fix, Nov, 16, 2016, <https://www.thecollegefix.com/post/29988/>
2. Warfel, R. H., *Noah Webster: Schoolmaster To America*, New Macmillan Company, 1936.
3. Proverbs 1:7

End Notes

4. *America's Skills Challenge: Millennials and the Future*, Educational Testing Services, 2015, https://www.ets.org/s/research/30079/asc-millennials-and-the-future.pdf
5. Snyder, Michael, *16 Facts That Prove America Is In Deep, Deep Trouble*, The Sleuth Journal, Aug. 2, 2017, <https://www.charismanews.com/opinion/66537-16-facts-that-prove-that-america-is-in-deep-deep-trouble>
6. Durden, Tyler, *America Hits Rock Bottom: Cities Are Paying Criminals $1000 Per Month "Not To Kill"*, Zerohedge.com, Mar. 28, 2016, <https://www.zerohedge.com/news/2016-03-28/america-hits-rock-bottom-cities-are-paying-criminals-1000-month-not-kill>
7. Fischer-Baum, Reuben, *Infographic: Is Your State's Highest-Paid Employee A Coach? (Probably)*, DeadSpin.com, May 9, 2013, <https://deadspin.com/infographic-is-your-states-highest-paid-employee-a-co-489635228>
8. Durdern, Tyler, *Depressing Survey Results Show How Extremely Stupid America Has Become*, Zerohedge.com, Mar. 30, 2016, <https://www.zerohedge.com/news/2016-03-30/depressing-survey-results-show-how-extremely-stupid-america-has-become>
9. *Where's Iraq: Young Adults Don't Know*, CBSNews.com, May 2, 2006, <https://www.cbsnews.com/news/wheres-iraq-young-adults-dont-know/>
10. Matthews, Blake, *Pornography should be treated like drink driving or teenage smoking, experts argue as they it is so widespread in U.S., it is a MAJOR health crisis*, May, 16, 2014, DailyMail.com, <https://www.dailymail.co.uk/news/article-2630438/Pornography-treated-like-drink-driving-teenager-smoking-experts-argue-widespread-U-S-MAJOR-health-crisis.html>
11. Proverbs 4:13

Day 13

1. Reagan, Ronald, 40th President of the United States, 1983.
2. Psalm 94:15
3. Psalm 9:15-16

Addendums

Day 14

1. Rev. Witherspoon, John, the Works of the Rev. John Witherspoon, Philadelphia: William Woodard, 1802, Vol. 111, p. 46.
2. Franklin, Benjamin, *The Works of Benjamin Franklin*, ed. Jared Sparks, Vol. pp. 281-282, to Thomas Paine.
3. O'Conner, John E., *William Paterson: Lawyer and Statesman*, p. 244, in a speech given on the Fourth of July, 1798.
4. Witherspoon, John, *The Works of John Witherspoon*, Vol. 3, p. 24, n.2, The Dominion of Providence Over the Passions of Men, May 17, 1776.
5. Adams, John Quincy, *An Answer to Pain's "Rights of Man"*, p. 13, 1793.
6. Grimaldi, Laura, "Lexington school calls cops on dad irate over gay books", *Boston Herald*, Apr. 28, 2005.
7. Huntington, Doug, "Bible Distributors File Lawsuit After Arrest, Police Bullying", *Christian Post*, Apr. 24, 2007 <http://christianpost.com/article/20070424/bible-distributors-file-lawsuit-after-arrest-police-bullying/index.html>
8. Goodstein, Laurie, "Disciplining of Student Is Defended: Gingrich Said Prayer Brought Punishment", *The Washington Post*, Dec. 6, 1994.
9. Ephesians 6:12-13
10. Acts 4:19-20

Day 15

1. Carroll, Charles, Signer of the Declaration of Independence, in a letter to James McHenry, 1800.
2. Judges 17:6
3. Proverbs 26:12

Day 16

1. Adams, Abigail, wife of John Adams, in a letter to Mercy Otis Warren, Nov. 5, 1775.
2. Eph. 3:10
3. Jer. 1:9-10
4. James 5:16

End Notes

   5. 2 Thess. 2:7
   6. 2 Cor. 10:4
   7. Heb 4:12-13

Day 17

1. Kent, James, Chief Justice New York Supreme Court, *People v. Ruggles*, 1811.
2. Mark 7:20-23
3. Adams, John Quincy, 6th President of the United States, *Letter of John Quincy Adams, to His Son, On the Bible and Its Teachings*, 1848.
4. John 8:31

Day 18

1. Kent, James, Chief Justice New York Supreme Court, *People v. Ruggles*, 1811.
2. Proverbs 12:3
3. 1 Timothy 2:1-4
4. John Adams, 2nd President of the United States, *The Works of John Adams*, Charles Francis Adams, editor (Boston: Charles C. Little and James Brown, 1851), Vol. IV, p. 56, "Novanglus: No. IV."

Day 19

1. Daniel Webster, Daniel, U.S. Congressman, U.S Senator, and U.S. Secretary of State, in a speech commemorating the 200-year anniversary of Pilgrims landing at Plymouth Rock, Dec. 22, 1820.
2. Massachusetts' Constitution, 1780, Part 1, Art. 3, drafted by John Adams, the world's oldest functioning written constitution.
3. Harry S. Truman, 39th President of the United States, address at the Cornerstone Laying of the New York Avenue Presbyterian Church, Apr. 3, 1961.
4. Proverbs 14:34

Addendums

Day 20

1. John Adams, 2nd President of the United States, *The Works of John Adams*, Charles Francis Adams, editor (Boston: Charles C. Little and James Brown, 1851), Vol. IV, p. 56, "Novanglus: No. IV."
2. Leviticus 18:21; 20:1-5; 2 Kings 21:2-6; Proverbs 6:16-17; Psalm 139:13-14; Jeremiah 7:30-31 (These are just a few.)
3. Matthew 6:32
4. Matthew 6:33

Day 21

1. Massachusetts' Constitution, 1780, Part 1, Art. 3, drafted by John Adams, the world's oldest functioning written constitution.
2. 1 Samuel 2 & 3

Day 22

1. Cleveland, Grover, 22nd and 24th President of the United States, Proclamation issued Oct. 25, 1887, setting aside Nov. 24, 1887 as Thanksgiving Day.
2. Santa Fe Independent School District v. Jane Doe, 2000.
3. 2 Chronicles 7:14
4. Mark 8:34

Day 23

1. Cass, Lewis, U.S. Secretary of State and Democratic presidential candidate, 1848.
2. Newdow v. United States, 2002; Newdow v. Rio Linda Union School District, 2014.
3. Matthew 16:24
4. Colossians 1:9-10
5. Daniel 9:13

End Notes

Day 24

1. Samuel Adams, *in an essay published in The Advertiser, 1748.*
2. Machiavelli, Niccolò, *The Prince*, 1513.

Day 25

1. Helvidius Priscus I (pen name of James Warren, President of the Massachusetts Provincial Congress) in an article in the Boston Independent Chronicle, Dec. 27, 1787.
2. Luke 11:8
3. Annie Laurie Gaylor, co-president of the Freedom From Religion Foundation, 1995.
4. Mark 16:20

Day 26

1. Lindsell, Harold, *The New Paganism*, San Francisco, Harper & Row, 1987, p. 213.
2. Matthew 16:15-18
3. Ephesians 2:20; 5:23
4. Matthew 7:24-27
5. John 3:16
6. 12:1-2; Rom 6:6-14
7. Leviticus 19:17
8. Leviticus 19:18
9. Martin Luther King, sermon delivered in 1957.
10. 1 Cor 13:4-8

Day 27

1. Thomas Paine, *American Crisis*, Dec. 1776.
2. Matthew 5:13-16
3. Thomas Paine, *American Crisis*, Dec. 1776.
4. Daniel 11:32

Addendums

Day 28

1. *Rules and Precepts*, the written purpose for higher education at Harvard University, 1638.
2. Flory v. Sioux Falls School District, 1979.
3. Matthew 18:6-7
4. Deuteronomy 11:18-19
5. Psalm 94:20; 119:126; 2 Kings 7:33
6. Romans 1:22

Day 29

1. Benjamin Rush, *Essays, Literary, Moral and Philosophical*, "Of the Mode of Education Proper in a Republic", p. 8, Thomas and William Bradford, Philadelphia, PA, 1806.
2. James Otis, *The Rights of the British Colonies Asserted and Proved*, pp. 11, 98, J. Williams and J. Almon, London, 1776.
3. John Adams, *The Works of John Adams, Second President of the United States*, in a letter to Zabdiel Adams on June 21, 1776, ed. Charles Francis Adams, Vol. IX, p. 401, Little, Brown, Boston, MA, 1854.
4. George Washington, *Address of George Washington, President of the United States... Preparatory to His Declination*, pp. 22-23, George and Henry S. Keatinge, 1796.
5. The American Dream, Investopedia, May 24, 2019. <https://www.investopedia.com/terms/a/american-dream.asp>
6. Matthew 6:33

Day 30

1. Monroe, James, 5th President of the United States, in his second State of the Nation address, Nov. 16, 1818.
2. Reed v. van Hoven, 1965.
3. Rush, Benjamin, signer of the Declaration of Independence, co-founder of five colleges, served under three Presidents, personally trained over 3,000 medical students, active in The Sons of Liberty, *Travels Through Life or Sundry Incidents in the Life of Dr. Benjamin Rush*, 1800.
4. Psalm 94:20; 119:126; 2 Kings 7:33

End Notes

5. Romans 1:22
6. Daniel 9:13

Day 31

1. John Quincy Adams, *Letters of John Quincy Adams to His Son on the Bible and Its Teachings* (Auburn: James M. Aiden, 1850), p. 34.
2. Stein v. Oshinsky, 1965; Collins v. Chandler Unified School District, 1981.
3. Psalm 111:10; Proverbs 1:7; 2:6; 9:10; 15:33; 21:30; 1 Corinthians 1:30; 2:16

Day 32

1. Noah Webster, *A Letter To A Young Gentleman*, 1823.

Day 33

1. Sciacca, Fran, *A Generation At Risk*, World Wide Publications, Minneapolis, MN, p. 130, 1990.
2. 1 Cor 2:4-5 Amplified Bible
3. Matt. 5:14-16 Amplified Bible
4. 2 Cor 6:17

Day 34

1. Daniel Webster, Daniel, U.S. Congressman, U.S Senator, and U.S. Secretary of State, in a speech commemorating the 200-year anniversary of Pilgrims landing at Plymouth Rock, Dec. 22, 1820.
2. Brewer, David, U.S Supreme Court Justice, *Church of the Holy Trinity v. United States*, 143 U.S. 457, 1892.
3. 2 Cor. 5:21
4. Luke 12:51-53; John 6:63-64; 8:32; 17:17-19
5. Lincoln, Abraham, 16th President of the United States, in a speech given in Springfield, IL, Jun. 16, 1858. See also: Matthew 12:25; Matthew. 7:24-27; Daniel 2:33-35

Addendums

Day 35

1. George Washington, 1ˢᵗ President of the United States, *Circular To The States*, Jun. 8, 1783.

Day 36

1. John Adams, in a letter to his cousin, Zabdiel Adams, June 21, 1776.
2. Luke 4:18
3. John 8:36
4. George Washington, 1ˢᵗ President of the United States, *Farewell Address*, printed in the American Daily Advertiser, Philadelphia, PA, Sep. 19, 1796.
5. Charles Carroll, signer of the Declaration of Independence, to James McHenry, Nov. 4, 1800.

Day 37

1. Tyler, John, 10ᵗʰ President of the United States, *Proclamation of a National Day of Fasting and Prayer*, Apr. 13, 1841.
2. Acts 4:18
3. Acts 4:29
4. Acts 4:19-20
5. Matthew 13:25

Day 38

1. Chase, Samuel, signer of the Declaration of Independence, U.S. Supreme Court Justice, Maryland Supreme Court Decision Runkel v, Winemiller, 1799
2. Fiano-Chesser, Cassy, *United Methodist Church proposes new belief statement: 'We support legal access to abortion'*, Aug. 28, 2018. <https://www.liveaction.org/news/united-methodist-church-removing-pro-life/>
3. Matt. 16:18; 7:24-27
4. Mark 16:20

End Notes

Day 39

1. Ezra Taft Benson, U.S. Secretary of Agriculture, *Americans Are Destroying America*, Apr. 1968.

Day 40

1. James A. Garfield, 23rd President of the United States, in a speech celebrating the 100the anniversary of the Declaration of Independence made while serving in Congress, Jul. 4, 1877.
2. Matt 16:24

Day 41

1. Bradley, General. Omar T, in a speech given on Armistice Day, Nov. 11, 1948.
2. Definition of 'scientism' from Dictionary.com
3. Matthew 7:20-23

Day 42

1. Washington, George, 1st President of the United States, in a conversation with his Vice-President John Adams, 1796, cited by Brian J. Buchannan, *Sex and Politics As News Is Hardly New,* First Amendment Center Online, Oct. 20, 2006.
2. Jefferson, Thomas, 3rd President of the United States, in a letter to John Norvell, Jun. 14, 1807.
3. Ibid.
4. Woodrow Wilson, 28th President of the United States, in a letter to Missouri Senator W. J. Stone, Mar. 1914.
5. 2 Peter 2:3
6. 2 Timothy 4:3-5
7. John 17:17
8. 2 Timothy 2:15-16

Addendums

Day 43

1. Bonhoeffer, Dietrich, *Letters and Papers From Prison*, written from 1943 to 1945 while in prison in Nazi Germany.
2. Ibid.
3. Eph. 5:13; Ps. 119:130
4. 2 Thessalonians 3:1
5. 1 Corinthians 14:8; Ephesians 5:11

Day 44

1. Report of the House Judiciary Committee, 1854, after a yearlong study on the issue of "the separation of church and state", B. F. Morris, *The Christian Life and Character of the Civil Institutions of the United States*, 1864, pg.328.
2. 1 Peter 1:24-25
3. Proverbs 22:20-21
4. Matthew 5:13
5. Finney, Charles, *The Decay Of Conscience*, The Independent of New York, December 4, 1873.

Day 45

1. William V. Wells, The Life and Public Service of Samuel Adams (Boston: Little, Brown, & Co., 1865), Vol. I, p. 22, quoting from a political essay by Samuel Adams published in The Public Advertiser, 1749.
2. James Madison, *The Papers of James Madison*, ed. Henry D. Gilpin (Langtree & O'Sullivan, Washington, 1840) Vol. III, p.1324, John Francis Mercer, Aug. 14, 1787,
3. Proverbs 29:2
4. Proverbs 28:12
5. Proverbs 28:28
6. Psalm 7:9

End Notes

Day 46

1. Noah Webster, *History of The United States*, 1832.
2. Proverbs 25:28

Day 47

1. Cooley, Thomas, President of the American Bar Association, *The General Principles of Constitutional Law in the United States of America*, ed. Andrew C. McLaughlin, 3rd ed., Boston: Little, Brown, and Company, 1898, pp. 224-25.
2. Jeremiah 6:16

Day 48

1. *Commissioners of Johnston County v. Lacy*, 93 S.E. 482, 487 (N.C. 1917).
2. *State v. City of Tampa*, 48 So.2d 78, 79 (Fla. 1950).
3. Noah Webster, *The History of the United States*, New Haven: Dury and Peck, 1833, p. 309.
4. *How Many Federal Laws Are There in the US*, Azarudeen, Abdul, Quora, Sep. 2, 2016, <https://www. quora.com/how-many-federal-laws-are-there-in-the-US>
5. John Quincy Adams, *Letters of John Quincy Adams to His Son*, p. 61, Charles Francis Adams, editor, Charles C. Little and James Brown, Boston, MA., 1871.
6. Wallace v. Jaffree, 1984
7. Galatians 5:14; Romans 13:10
8. Noah Webster, *The History of the United States*, New Haven: Dury and Peck, 1833, p. 309.

Day 49

1. Matthew 15:19-20
2. Paul Johnson, *A History of the American People*, 1997

Addendums

3. Edwards, Johnathan, an account of the effects of the Great Awakening in Northhampton, MA in a letter to Rev. Thomas Prince of Boston, Dec. 12, 1743.

Day 50

1. Roosevelt, Theodore, 26th President of the United States, as quoted by George Grant, The Quick and The Dead, Crossway, Wheaton, IL, 1984, p. 134.
2. Ecclesiastes 4:12
3. Matt 18:19-20
4. 2 Timothy 3:16-17

Day 51

1. Franklin, Benjamin, an address on prayer at the Consitituional Convention, Philadelphia, PA, Jun. 28, 1787.
2. John 17:3
3. Romans 10:17
4. Ephesians 5:13; Psalm 119:130
5. Ephesians 5:26
6. DeLoss Love, *The Fast and Thanksgiving Days of New England*, Fast and Thanksgiving Days Calendar, pp. 464-514, Boston, MA, Houghton, Mifflin and Company, 1895.

Day 52

1. Webster, Daniel, *The Dignity and Importance of History*, an address delivered before the New York Historical Society, Feb. 23, 1852.
2. Luke 6:46-49

Day 53

1. Story, Joseph, U.S. Supreme Court Justice, *A Familiar Exposition of the Constitution of the United States, 1840*.

End Notes

2. Holmes, Jr. Oliver Wendell, Collected Legal Papers, *'The Law in Science – Science in Law"*, Harcourt, Brace, and Howe, New York, 1920.
3. Cardozo, Benjamin, *The Growth of the Law*, Yale University Press, New Haven, CT, 1924.
4. Cardozo, Benjamin, *The Nature of the Judicial Process*, Yale University Press, New Haven, CT, 1921.
5. Hughes, Charles Evans, *The Autobiographical Notes of Charles Evans Hughes,* ed. David J. Danelski, Speech at Elmira, May 3, 1907, Harvard University Press, Cambridge, 1973.

Day 54

1. Lincoln, Abraham, 16th President of the United States, Notes for a Speech in Kansas and Ohio, Sep. 1859.
2. Psalm 119:126
3. Ephesians 6:12-18

Day 55

1. *Adams, Samuel, The Boston Gazette, Apr. 4, 1768.*
2. Jehle, Dr. Paul, Executive Director of Plymouth Rock Foundation, *Six Steps To Freedom, The Pilgrim's Legacy of Economic Liberty,* The Founder's Bible, pp.1581-1589, Shiloh Road Publishers, LLC, 2012.
3. Jefferson, Thomas, 3rd President of the United States, *The Writings of Thomas Jefferson,* ed. Albert E. Bergh, Thomas Jefferson Memorial Association, Washington, 1904.

Day 56

1. Story, Joseph, U.S. Supreme Court Justice, commenting on the pamphlet The Relation of Christianity to the Civil Government of the United States, 1833.

Addendums

Day 57

1. Jay, John, The Life of John Jay, With Selections of His Correspondence and Miscellaneous Papers, ed. William Jay, "At the Annual Meeting, May 8, 1823", p. 503, J & J Harper, New York, 1833.
2. Love, DeLoss, *The Fast and Thanksgiving Days of New England*, pp. 464-514, "Fast and Thanksgiving Days Calendar", Houghton, Mifflin and Company, Boston, MA, 1895.
3. Luke 11:2-4
4. Psalm 94:20

Day 58

1. Samuel Adams, in an essay published in *The Advertiser*, 1748.
2. Psalm 80:3
3. 2 Corinthians 6:1
4. Whittaker Chambers, *Witness,* Washington: Regnery Gateway, 1952.
5. George Washington, *Address of George Washington, President of the United States... Preparatory to His Declination*, Baltimore: George and Henry S. Keatings, 1796, pp. 22-23.
6. 2 Chronicles 7:14

Day 59

1. Alexis de Tocqueville, *Democracy In America*, 1835.
2. Lutz, Donald S., "The Relative Influence of European Writers on Late Eighteenth Century American Political Thought", *American Political Science Review*, Vol. 78, Issue 1, pp. 191-193, Mar. 1984.
3. Webster, Noah, *Preface to Noah Webster's Dictionary*, 1928.

Day 60

1. Daniel Webster, U.S. Senator from Massachusetts 1845-1850, Secretary of State 1850-1852, lawyer. "The Voices of America's Heritage," *Torch* (Dallas, TX: Texas Eagle Forum, February 1994), vol. 1, no. 7, p. 4.
2. Herlong, Albert S., Democratic Congressman from FL, Congressional Record, January 10, 1963.

End Notes

3. Benjamin Rush, *Essays, Literary, Moral & Philosophical*, (Thomas & Samuel F. Bradford, Philadelphia, 1798, pp. 93, A Defense of the Use of the Bible as a School Book, Addressed to the Rev. Jeremy Belknap of Boston, Mar. 10, 1791.

Addendum A: Prayer Prepper's Call To Action, Part 1

1. Genesis 1:2
2. Matthew 8:8
3. Psalm 146:3-4
4. Isaiah 1:25-26; 33:6
5. Daniel 9:13
6. Luke 1:16-17

Addendum A: Prayer Prepper's Call To Action, Part 2

1. 1 Timothy 6:10
2. Psalm 146:3-4
3. Isaiah 1:25-26; 33:6
4. Daniel 9:13
5. Luke 1:16-17

Addendum A: Prayer Prepper's Call To Action, Part 3

1. John 3:19
2. Psalm 94:15
3. Stanton, Glenn, *Is Biblical Christianity on the Decline?*, Focus On The Family, <https://www.focusonthefamily.com/about/focus-findings/religion-and-culture/is-biblical-christianity-on-the-decline>
4. Genesis 18:22-32
5. Psalm 146:3-4
6. Isaiah 1:25-26; 33:6
7. Daniel 9:13
8. Luke 1:16-17

Addendums

Addendum A: Election Day
1. Proverbs 17:17
2. James Madison, in an address to the General Assembly of the State of Virginia, 1778.
3. Benjamin Rush, *Essays, Literary, Moral and Philosophical*, "Of the Mode of Education Proper in a Republic", p. 8, Thomas and William Bradford, Philadelphia, PA, 1806.
4. Exodus 20:7
5. Webster, Daniel, *The Dignity and Importance of History, an address delivered before the New York Historical Society, Feb. 23, 1852.*

Addendum B: Thanksgiving Day
1. 1 Peter 1:1
2. Hebrews 11:13
3. 1 Peter 2:11-12
4. Romans 12:1-2
5. Matthew 15:19-20
6. John 8:32
7. 2 Corinthians 9:11
8. Acts 4:29-30
9. Daniel 9:13

Addendum C: Scriptures
1. John 17:3
2. 2 Timothy 3:16-17
3. Acts 4:24-30
4. John 1:5
5. Isaiah 55:11
6. Acts 17: 6
7. James 5:16

www.ingramcontent.com/pod-product-compliance
Lightning Source LLC
Chambersburg PA
CBHW080912170426
43201CB00017B/2297